Date Due

D1442201

KING PHILIP

NORTH AMERICAN INDIANS OF ACHIEVEMENT

KING PHILIP
Wampanoag Rebel

▼▼▼

Joseph Roman

Senior Consulting Editor
W. David Baird
Howard A. White Professor of History
Pepperdine University

CHELSEA HOUSE PUBLISHERS

Philadelphia

FRONTISPIECE   An oil painting of King Philip from 1893. The painting is now housed in the Haffenreffer Museum of Anthropology in Bristol, Rhode Island.

ON THE COVER   An illustration of King Philip. The figure's clothing is adapted from a portrait of Philip, painted circa 1850. The facial features are based on late-19th- and early-20th-century photographs of Philip's descendants.

Chelsea House Publishers

EDITOR-IN-CHIEF   Remmel Nunn
MANAGING EDITOR   Karyn Gullen Browne
COPY CHIEF   Mark Rifkin
PICTURE EDITOR   Adrian G. Allen
ART DIRECTOR   Maria Epes
ASSISTANT ART DIRECTOR   Noreen Romano
MANUFACTURING MANAGER   Gerald Levine
SYSTEMS MANAGER   Lindsey Ottman
PRODUCTION MANAGER   Joseph Romano
PRODUCTION COORDINATOR   Marie Claire Cebrián

North American Indians of Achievement

SENIOR EDITOR   Liz Sonneborn

Staff for KING PHILIP

COPY EDITOR   Benson D. Simmonds
EDITORIAL ASSISTANT   Michele Haddad
DESIGNER   Debora Smith
PICTURE RESEARCHERS   Diana Gongora, Sandy Jones
COVER ILLUSTRATION   Janet Hamlin

3 5 7 9 8 6 4

Library of Congress Cataloging-in-Publication Data

Roman, Joseph.
King Philip/by Joseph Roman
p. cm.—(North American Indians of Achievement)
Includes bibliographical references and index.
Summary: Examines the life and career of the 17th-century Wampanoag Indian chief.
ISBN 0-7910-1704-4
1. Philip, Sachem of the Wampanoags, d. 1676—Juvenile literature. 2. Wampanoag Indians—Biography—Juvenile literature. 2. Wampanoag Indians—Kings and rulers—Juvenile literature. 4. King Philip's War, 1675–76—Juvenile literature. [1. Philip, Sachem of the Wampanoags, d. 1676. 2. Wampanoag Indians—Biography. 3. Native Americans of Achievement—Biography. 4. King Philip's War, 1675–76.] I. Title. II. Series.
E99.W2P487 1991   91-2331
973.2'4'092—dc20   CIP
[B]   AC

CONTENTS

NORTH AMERICAN INDIANS OF ACHIEVEMENT

BLACK HAWK
Sac Rebel

JOSEPH BRANT
Mohawk Chief

COCHISE
Apache Chief

CRAZY HORSE
Sioux War Chief

CHIEF GALL
Sioux War Chief

GERONIMO
Apache Warrior

HIAWATHA
Founder of the Iroquois
Confederacy

CHIEF JOSEPH
Nez Percé Leader

PETER MACDONALD
Former Chairman of the Navajo
Nation

WILMA MANKILLER
Principal Chief of the Cherokees

OSCEOLO
Seminole Rebel

QUANAH PARKER
Comanche Chief

KING PHILIP
Wampanoag Rebel

**POCAHONTAS AND CHIEF
POWHATAN**
Leaders of the Powhatan Tribes

PONTIAC
Ottawa Rebel

RED CLOUD
Sioux War Chief

WILL ROGERS
Cherokee Entertainer

SEQUOYAH
Inventor of the Cherokee Alphabet

SITTING BULL
Chief of the Sioux

TECUMSEH
Shawnee Rebel

JIM THORPE
Sac and Fox Athlete

SARAH WINNEMUCCA
Northern Paiute Writer and
Diplomat

Other titles in preparation

ON INDIAN LEADERSHIP

by W. David Baird
Howard A. White Professor of History
Pepperdine University

Authoritative utterance is in thy mouth, perception is in thy heart, and thy tongue is the shrine of justice," the ancient Egyptians said of their king. From him, the Egyptians expected authority, discretion, and just behavior. Homer's *Iliad* suggests that the Greeks demanded somewhat different qualities from their leaders: justice and judgment, wisdom and counsel, shrewdness and cunning, valor and action. It is not surprising that different people living at different times should seek different qualities from the individuals they looked to for guidance. By and large, a people's requirements for leadership are determined by two factors: their culture and the unique circumstances of the time and place in which they live.

Before the late 15th century, when non-Indians first journeyed to what is now North America, most Indian tribes were not ruled by a single person. Instead, there were village chiefs, clan headmen, peace chiefs, war chiefs, and a host of other types of leaders, each with his or her own specific duties. These influential people not only decided political matters but also helped shape their tribe's social, cultural, and religious life. Usually, Indian leaders held their positions because they had won the respect of their peers. Indeed, if a leader's followers at any time decided that he or she was out of step with the will of the people, they felt free to look to someone else for advice and direction.

Thus, the greatest achievers in traditional Indian communities were men and women of extraordinary talent. They were not only skilled at navigating the deadly waters of tribal politics and cultural customs but also able to, directly or indirectly, make a positive and significant difference in the daily life of their followers.

7

From the beginning of their interaction with Native Americans, non-Indians failed to understand these features of Indian leadership. Early European explorers and settlers merely assumed that Indians had the same relationship with their leaders as non-Indians had with their kings and queens. European monarchs generally inherited their positions and ruled large nations however they chose, often with little regard for the desires or needs of their subjects. As a result, the settlers of Jamestown saw Pocahontas as a "princess" and Pilgrims dubbed Wampanoag leader Metacom "King Philip," envisioning them in roles very different from those in which their own people placed them.

As more and more non-Indians flocked to North America, the nature of Indian leadership gradually began to change. Influential Indians no longer had to take on the often considerable burden of pleasing only their own people; they also had to develop a strategy of dealing with the non-Indian newcomers. In a rapidly changing world, new types of Indian role models with new ideas and talents continually emerged. Some were warriors; others were peacemakers. Some held political positions within their tribes; others were writers, artists, religious prophets, or athletes. Although the demands of Indian leadership altered from generation to generation, several factors that determined which Indian people became prominent in the centuries after first contact remained the same.

Certain personal characteristics distinguished these Indians of achievement. They were intelligent, imaginative, practical, daring, shrewd, uncompromising, and logical. They were constant in friendships, unrelenting in hatreds, affectionate with their relatives, and respectful to their God or gods. Of course, no single Native American leader embodied all these qualities, nor these qualities only. But it was these characteristics that allowed them to succeed.

The special skills and talents that certain Indians possessed also brought them to positions of importance. The life of Hiawatha, the legendary founder of the powerful Iroquois Confederacy, displays the value that oratorical ability had for many Indians in power. The biography of Cochise, the 19th-century Apache chief, illustrates that leadership often required keen diplomatic skills not only in transactions among tribespeople but also in hardheaded negotiations with non-Indians. For others, such as Mohawk Joseph Brant and Navajo Peter MacDonald, a non-Indian education proved advantageous in their dealings with other peoples.

Sudden changes in circumstance were another crucial factor in determining who became influential in Indian communities. King Philip in the 1670s and Geronimo in the 1880s both came to power when their people were searching for someone to lead them into battle against white frontiersmen who had forced upon them a long series of indignities. Seeing the rising discontent of Indians of many tribes in the 1810s, Tecumseh and his brother, the Shawnee prophet Tenskwatawa, proclaimed a message of cultural revitalization that appealed to thousands. Other Indian achievers recognized cooperation with non-Indians as the most advantageous path during their lifetime. Sarah Winnemucca in the late 19th century bridged the gap of understanding between her people and their non-Indian neighbors through the publication of her autobiography *Life Among the Piutes*. Olympian Jim Thorpe in the early 20th century championed the assimilationist policies of the U.S. government and, with his own successes, demonstrated the accomplishments Indians could make in the non-Indian world. And Wilma Mankiller, principal chief of the Cherokees, continues to fight successfully for the rights of her people through the courts and through negotiation with federal officials.

Leadership among Native Americans, just as among all other peoples, can be understood only in the context of culture and history. But the centuries that Indians have had to cope with invasions of foreigners in their homelands have brought unique hardships and obstacles to the Native American individuals who most influenced and inspired others. Despite these challenges, there has never been a lack of Indian men and women equal to these tasks. With such strong leaders, it is no wonder that Native Americans remain such a vital part of this nation's cultural landscape.

1

"SO THE WAR BEGUN WITH PHILIP"

On June 30, 1675, a group of English colonists marched across the Mount Hope peninsula of present-day Rhode Island. They were heading deep into the territory of the Wampanoag Indians. Wampanoag warriors had been raiding the farms on the outskirts of the English town of Swansea for several days. But the colonists did not fight back against the raiders. They preferred to wait until they had gathered sufficient troops to confront the estimated 1,000 warriors that King Philip, the leader of the Wampanoags, had assembled at Mount Hope.

The small army, flanked by horsemen to protect them from an ambush, marched down the hot dirt road. They were not looking forward to the battle. Stopping suddenly, one of the soldiers fired at a movement in a nearby bush and hit one of his own men. The man suffered only a flesh wound, but the accident exposed the nervousness felt by all.

Soon the army came upon a shocking sight. "After the barbarous manner of the savages," wrote one chronicler, the heads, scalps, and hands of eight English settlers had been impaled on posts. Full of dread, the men removed the grisly remains and continued on.

A 19th-century engraving of King Philip.

As they approached the Wampanoag village, their spirits began to lift. There was no sign of King Philip or his tribe; the village was deserted. It appeared that Philip had seen the oncoming troops and fled. Believing that they had captured the enemy's land without having to fire a single shot and without losing even one man, some of the colonists began to cheer and "not a few pleased themselves with the fancy of a mighty conquest."

These were the mocking words of Benjamin Church, a young soldier who had met with Philip's warriors before. He later wrote about his experiences in his book *Entertaining Passages Relating to King Philip's War.* Church knew that Philip would not give up his land so easily. Prepared for a war, he tried to convince the other men to go after Philip. But having "conquered" Philip's homeland with little effort, the soldiers voted to build a fort instead. That way they could avoid facing a dangerous fight. Church urged the men to stop Philip now, before he could gather more allies. Looking at the discarded war drums Philip and his counselors had used to incite support, Church felt sure that the colonists would soon see battles far worse than any they might have faced that day. And he was right.

A few days earlier, Philip had stood at the edge of his village, watching as his tribespeople stepped into their canoes and paddled off into the bay. They had spent an entire day packing up their belongings. The women had cleared out the wigwams and collected their baskets and other supplies. The men in traditional battle dress—their faces painted, their bodies oiled with grease, and their black crests of hair pointing upward—carried their guns and tomahawks. They were well prepared for war.

The long, sturdy canoes silently crossed the dark water of Mount Hope Bay and entered the Pocasset swamp. Philip would not fight in his own village, where Wam-

A 19th-century engraving of Philip's 1675 escape from Mount Hope.

panoag women and children might be slaughtered by the approaching army. He knew that the soldiers would be reluctant to pursue them into the swamps. They were more likely to wait for a confrontation on dry land or to try to persuade another Indian tribe to join them before going to battle in the swamp. Either way, the war now seemed inevitable. As the colonists had clearly stated, it was too late for negotiation.

Several weeks earlier, as Philip had been preparing his men for the possibility of war, a group of Englishmen from the colony of Rhode Island had come to implore him to settle his differences with the Plymouth colonists peacefully. In the less than 50 years since English immigrants had founded Plymouth Colony, these settlers had caused many problems for Philip and his people. The Rhode Islanders convinced a reluctant Philip to meet with them. But then John Easton, the deputy governor of Rhode Island, received a letter from Plymouth saying that the colonists there refused to talk with Philip. They insisted that the Wampanoags could be dealt with only by force.

Since becoming sachem, or chief, Philip had demonstrated that he was not as eager to please the colonists as his father, Massasoit, had been. For almost a decade, Massasoit had readily accepted the terms that the Plymouth General Court had forced upon him. But the restrictions forbidding the sale of Wampanoag land to other colonies and the heavy fines the court demanded for breaking these rules left Philip with no choice but to disobey. His father's subservience had not won power for his people. His counselors had warned him that the first settlers would be followed by many more, but Philip's father disregarded their advice and allowed the newcomers to gain increasing strength. It was now left to Philip to try a more severe strategy.

The tension between the colonists at Plymouth and the Wampanoags had been growing for some time. In one incident, the body of John Sassamon, a Christian Indian, was found with a broken neck beneath the ice of Assawompsett Pond. Sassamon was a known informer who had fought with the English against the Pequot Indians years before. He had just reported to Plymouth governor Josiah Winslow that Philip was preparing for a war against the colonists when he disappeared.

In early June of 1675, three Wampanoags were seized and charged with committing Sassoman's murder. Among them were Tobias, one of Philip's counselors, and his son Wampapaquin. Despite a lack of evidence, a Plymouth jury found the men guilty. Several Christian Indians sat with the jury in an attempt to make the trial appear fair. The Indians, however, were not allowed to vote or in any way affect the verdict.

None of the Wampanoags admitted their guilt during the trial. But after two of the Indians had been hanged, the rope placed around the neck of Wampapaquin broke and he fell to the ground beneath the gallows. Shocked and terrified, the youth confessed that the three Indians had conspired in the affair and blamed the two dead Indians for the actual murder. Perhaps he was encouraged to speak by an offer of freedom from Plymouth officials. But in any case, after his confession was recorded by the court, he was quickly shot before he could take back his words.

And now, without any orders from Philip, fighting had erupted. A few of the more militant warriors in his tribe plundered a house near Swansea, which was built on land that Philip believed belonged to him. One of the warriors was shot when he was caught ransacking a settler's house. Later, some Wampanoags went to Swansea, and a group of settlers asked them if the warrior had died. During the conversation, an English boy interrupted, saying that it didn't matter whether the man was dead or not, since he was only an Indian after all. Despite the protests of the older settlers, the Indians stormed off angrily. Later that night, without consulting Philip, the Indians attacked the farm and killed the young boy and his father. They were eager to avenge the abuses they had suffered for so many years at the hands of the settlers.

After the incident on the farm, Philip expected even greater retaliation from the colonists. He decided to leave his homeland at Montaup, or Mount Hope, as the settlers called it. He would take refuge with his sister-in-law, Weetamoo, the sachem of the Pocasset tribe.

Philip pushed out into the darkness, across waters black as crows' wings. The recent displays of bloodshed and aggression were not the only factors contributing to the desperate situation of his people. Changes had been occurring throughout Philip's life. In the course of only a few decades, the English settlers had come to think of the Indians' land as their own sacred home. It did not matter to these newcomers that the Wampanoags and other Indian nations had been there beyond all memory. Perhaps, as the region's deer, bears, and beavers were replaced by the settlers' cows, pigs, and horses, the Wampanoags themselves would be replaced by the growing number of settlers.

The colonists were much better armed than Philip's men, but the young sachem recognized that he would have to fight not only the colonists' weapons but also the changes in his own people. What little game was available in the region was no longer hunted simply for food. The Wampanoag men now hunted animals in order to trade the skins to the colonists for duffel, a coarse woolen cloth that the Indians had begun to wear instead of valuable skins. They also traded for wampum (beads made from polished shells) and other goods.

Even Philip treasured the goods the colonists traded. But no matter how much duffel or how many wampum belts he amassed, his power was still severely limited. Over the past ten years since he had become sachem, Philip had signed three treaties with Plymouth Colony. The settlers had promised "no English trouble" in

An illustration of Philip's home, Mount Hope (shown here in the background), as it appeared in the mid-19th century.

exchange for his promise not to sell any of his land to other colonies. But then Plymouth colonists settled on the edge of Wampanoag land, establishing the town called Swansea. Each year the town's population grew. The English farms began using more and more Indian land, and the settlers' livestock often encroached on Wampanoag cornfields. With so many settlers nearby, English trouble seemed unavoidable.

So Philip defied Plymouth and sold land to the settlers at Providence. His refusal to comply with Plymouth's every wish led to resentment and fear in the colony.

Philip's canoe was one of the last to reach the bank of Weetamoo's village. Weetamoo welcomed him and his people into her tribe. Sweltering heat, swarms of fierce mosquitoes, and the threat of rattlesnake bites made life almost unbearable in the swamp. But as Philip slogged up the bank, he felt secure that his wife and child and the rest of his tribe would be safe here, at least for a little while.

As his men organized themselves into small parties, preparing to hide in the depths of the "abode of owls," as the Indians called the swamp, he realized that he would have to consider the actions of other nearby tribes. Although there was no alliance between his tribe and the powerful Narragansetts, the war he planned to wage against Plymouth Colony might well attract them. Unfortunately, he could not be sure on which side they would fight. If the Narragansetts stayed neutral, perhaps the colonists in Connecticut and Rhode Island would avoid the war as well. And then the Wampanoags would stand a better chance.

During the massacre of the Pequot Indians, which occurred in 1637, the English did not spare women and children when they attacked. They killed everyone in sight with a hard-heartedness that the Indians had never

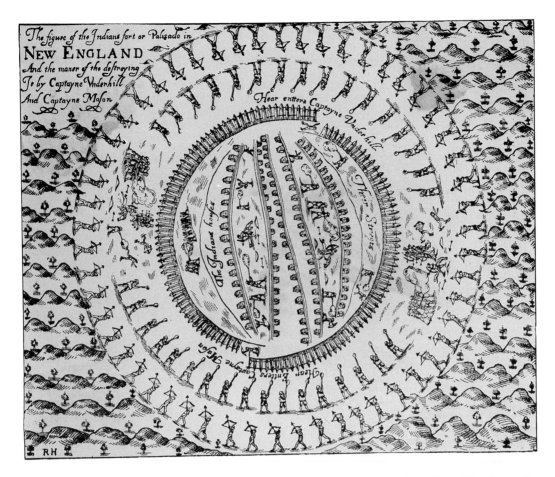

The figure of the Indians fort or Palizado in NEW ENGLAND And the maner of the destroying It by Captayne Vnderhill And Captayne Mason

Hear entters Captayne Vnderhill

The Indians houses

Their Streets

Hear entters Captayne Mason

RH

A diagram of the fort of the Pequot Indians that was originally printed in News from America, *a 1638 book by Captain John Underhill that related the history of the English colonies in North America. Underhill commanded the English forces that had attacked the Pequots the previous year.*

seen before, almost annihilating the tribe. The few who survived escaped to neighboring tribes to the north or were taken off in boats to be sold as slaves. After the English withdrew, all that remained of the Pequot homeland was a destroyed village littered with unburied corpses.

Philip stood on the bank looking out at the brightening sky. His first step would be to ensure the safety of the women and children. Then he and his warriors would be free to cross the plains under cover of night and attack nearby towns and villages where and when they wished. The war that he was about to enter would become one of the most devastating in New England history. It was not a battle that could be fought halfway.

The interior of a Wampanoag dwelling at Plimouth Plantation in Plymouth, Massachusetts. An outdoor museum, Plimouth Plantation includes a modern reconstruction of a 17th-century Indian village.

2

DIVINE PROVIDENCE

The Wampanoags kept no written records. But Philip learned much about their history from his father and other elders in the tribe. He knew how his people had lived before the first colonists arrived. And he understood the vast changes that had occurred in Wampanoag culture through interactions with the colonists even before he was born. As sachem, he considered this knowledge carefully before deciding to go to war.

Before the first English explorers reached the shores of what they would later call New England, the Wampanoag Indians numbered between 21,000 and 24,000 and lived at the head of what is now Narragansett Bay, between the present-day cities of Fall River, Massachusetts, and Providence, Rhode Island. (Today the term Wampanoags refers to a group of Indians living throughout southeastern Massachusetts.) The Wampanoags were one tribe within the vast group of Algonkian people who lived throughout the region. The Algonkians shared similar cultures and beliefs and spoke related languages.

The Wampanoags and most of the other Algonkian tribes lived in villages that were inhabited by a few hundred people. Daniel Gookin, the superintendent of the Indians in Massachusetts Bay Colony, described the wigwams in which they lived as being "built with small poles fixed in the ground, bent and fastened together with barks of trees oval or arbor-wise on the top." Covered with bark or mats made of sewn cattails or woven bulrushes, the wigwams were easy to move each season, when the tribe changed locations in search of better hunting or fishing. Mobility was an important part of their life, so the Indians had few possessions. As Thomas Morton, an Englishman who lived among the Indians, said: "They love not to bee cumbered with many utensilles."

The Wampanoags relied primarily on agriculture for their food. They grew crops, including corn, beans, tobacco, and gourds, in the fertile soil of their homeland.

A wooden bowl made by the Wampanoags in the mid-17th century. It is believed to have been owned by King Philip.

The women were responsible for raising all the crops except tobacco, which was grown exclusively by men. Using hoes made from shells and wood, the Indian women grew their crops in large quantities. Roger Williams, a clergyman who defended Indians' rights for much of his life, described the women's work: "[They] constantly beat all their corne with hand: they plant it, dresse it, gather it, barne it, beat it, and take as much paines as any people in the world."

Although corn constituted a large part of the Indians' diet, beans were an important supplement. Both corn and beans were stored for the winter. The women often prepared the corn by simply boiling it and serving it with kidney beans. They also made *nokake*, a ground parched corn that Wampanoag warriors carried into the forest on hunting expeditions. Daniel Gookin was so taken with this cake that he wrote:

> It is so sweet, toothsome, and hearty, that an Indian will travel many days with no other food but this meal, which he eateth as he need, and after it drinketh water. And for this end, when they travel a journey, or go a hunting, they carry this nokake in a basket, or bag, for their use.

At home, nokake was often served as a porridge.

According to Wampanoag legend, the great provider of this wealth of food was the supreme god, Cautantowwit, who lived in the Southwest, where the good, warm weather came from. The crow was Cautantowwit's messenger. It was said that the crow, traveling from the Southwest, carried a kernel of corn and a bean in each ear and dispersed them among the northern tribes. Although all animals were sacred to the Indians, the crow was especially revered.

In Wampanoag culture, maintaining a life of abundance and health required sacrifices and rituals. Unlike corn and beans, which were foods the Indians could grow in unlimited quantities, meat was naturally limited by the number of animals available for hunting. At times during winter when snow did not cover the ground, animal tracking became difficult. Some years the Indians had so little food that they faced starvation. But even when the hunt was successful, the slaughter of an animal often required an act of thanksgiving to its spirit. For example, after the fur and meat were taken from a beaver to help clothe and feed a family, the animal's bones had to be protected and returned to its native stream.

The Wampanoags did not kill more animals than was absolutely necessary. To do so would upset the spiritual balance they held with all living things in the forest and on the plains. If the Indians lived a good life, not only would Cautantowwit provide more power, health, and food, but they could also expect to go to the lands of the Southwest when they died. There, they would live in endless warmth and pleasure.

When English settlers first arrived in the region, they were surprised by the abundance of available fish and game. In their writings, they reported that smelts, alewives, sturgeon, and other ocean fishes were so numerous that when they migrated to fresh water to spawn it was possible to walk across the streams and rivers on the fish's backs. Birds, too, were very plentiful. The settlers reported that half a dozen wild turkeys could be killed a day. English traveler John Josselyn wrote of the huge flocks of passenger pigeons that migrated twice a year "that in my thinking [they] had neither beginning nor ending, length nor breadth and [flew] so thick that I could see no Sun."

Perhaps most dramatic of all were the reports of wild animals that roamed through Algonkian territory. William Wood, an early settler of Boston, described in verse the various animals he saw:

> The kingly Lyon, and the strong arm'd Beare
> The large limbed Mooses, with the tripping Deare,
> Quill darting Porcupine, and Rakcoones bee,
> Castelld in the hollow of an aged tree;
> The skipping Squerrell, Rabbet, purblinde Hare,
> Immured in the selfsame Castle are,
> Least red-eyed Ferrets, wily Foxes should
> Them undermine, if rampird but with mould
> The grim fac't Ounce, and ravenous Woolfe,
> Whose meager paunch sucks like a swallowing gulfe.
> Black glistering Otters, and rich coated Bever . . .

Wood continued that he had never actually seen any lions in the forest, but had heard of their existence in the north.

The forests of coastal New England in which the Indians placed their snares and hunted with bows and arrows were thick with oak, hickory, chestnut, hemlock, walnut, and white pine trees. Many Indians lived in the swamps along the rocky shores and on wide, clear plains. Well-worn trails traversed these different environments, connecting the Wampanoag with nearby tribes.

By avoiding unwarranted hunting and establishing a spiritual balance with nature, the Wampanoags maintained a fairly constant food supply. A political balance with neighboring tribes allowed them to live relatively peacefully. But the balance in their lives was thrown off by the arrival of European settlers.

When Philip's father, Massasoit, was still a young man, he heard of a strange ship that had anchored offshore in sight of the Patuxet tribe's traditional lands (later to be renamed Plymouth). The Patuxets gathered along the beach to greet the dark-robed men on board. British captain Thomas Hunt and his men had come to trade goods at an Indian village. But just before leaving, Hunt ordered his men to capture some Indians, hoping to sell them at the slave markets in Spain.

TRADITIONAL TRIBAL TERRITORIES IN SOUTHERN NEW ENGLAND

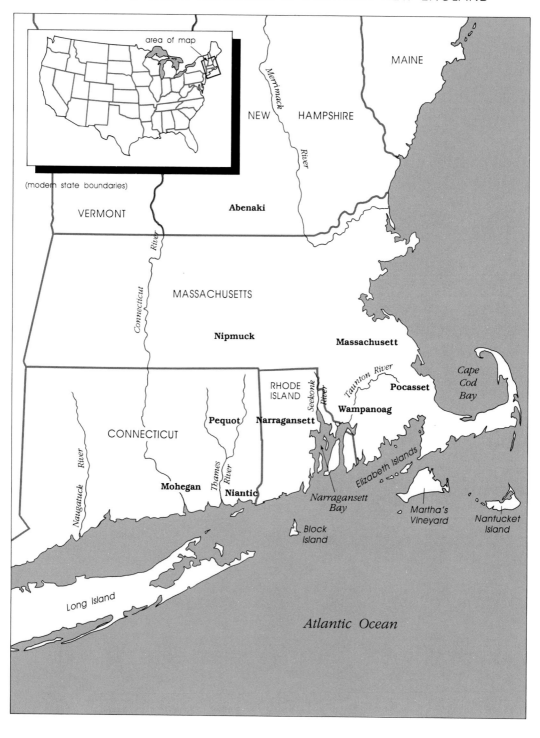

From this first meeting, the Indians learned to distrust the strangers from across the sea. But in the years to follow, white men would leave them with something far more devastating than mistrust. In 1616, epidemics ravaged the tribes in the north. By 1618, European diseases had spread among the Patuxets and many nearby tribes, posing a serious threat to the future of the Indians in the region.

The loss of life was so great among the Wampanoags that the tribe soon bypassed their formal burial rights and started digging mass grave sites. As the number of deaths increased, some tribespeople were even left unburied, causing further anxiety that the spirits of the departed might take offense. The victims of the disease were often stranded by the rest of the tribe, who fled in terror at new outbreaks of illness.

Disease not only destroyed most of the population from Cape Cod to Penobscot Bay but also greatly diminished the political strength of the survivors. Relatively untouched by the new diseases, the nearby Narragansett tribe took advantage of the epidemics suffered by their neighbors by taking control of their territories and villages. As the survivors of the other tribes joined together to defend themselves against the Narragansetts, a man named Massasoit became the leader of many of the Wampanoags who withstood the epidemics.

To the defeated tribes, who believed that even an everyday accident was caused by their god's anger, the Narragansetts' health could only have meant one thing: Their sacrifices to Cautantowwit, including destroying property in honor of the creator, had succeeded where their own rituals had failed. After an incident in which the Narragansetts brutally murdered a Patuxet sachem, Massasoit quickly humbled himself to the powerful tribe, offering to leave Narragansett Bay and settle near the

Taunton River if they would spare his life and allow his people to leave. The Narragansetts accepted his plea and let the sachem resettle farther north.

In the midst of the epidemics, other non-Indian foreigners arrived in Wampanoag territory. This time they did not come merely to trade or to hunt for slaves. These people were Puritans searching for a new land where they could find refuge from the intolerance of the Church of England. Unlike the earlier traders, these strangers had permanent settlement in mind. The Puritans, or Pilgrims as they are now commonly known, landed at the abandoned village of the Patuxets. They were pleasantly surprised to see the area cleared of native inhabitants.

But their pleasure was short-lived, as half of the newly arrived English population died during their first harsh winter. Despite the seemingly endless supply of timber for fuel and building materials—so scarce in Old England—the newly arrived men and women were

An engraving of the Pilgrims' landing at Plymouth in 1620.

unprepared for the hardships of the cold. Their temporary shelters were hastily built and rarely watertight. Lacking proper provisions for the winter and adequate knowledge of the region for hunting, the settlers went hungry without help from the Indians.

Fear and the suspicion that the strangers were the cause of the mysterious deaths among the Indians kept the Wampanoags and other tribes away from the Patuxet village for the long winter months. But with the arrival of spring, an Abenaki chief named Samoset strode into the small village of foreigners. He spent the night with the settlers and left the following day with a bracelet, a ring, and a knife given to him as gifts. He promised to return with more Indians and skins for trading. On his second visit, he brought Squanto, one of the first Indians who came to trust the settlers. Squanto was already well acquainted with the English. He had been captured years before at the Patuxet village by Captain Thomas Hunt. Somehow he managed to escape from Spain, where Hunt had attempted to sell him as a slave, and get to London. In March 1619, he left England with Captain Thomas Dermer to return to Patuxet territory. Arriving back in his native land, he left Dermer's service to search for his tribe.

The Patuxet Indians had been completely decimated by disease in his absence, so Squanto was forced to join the Wampanoags as an outsider. The arrival of the English settlers gave him an opportunity to form an important alliance with the Pilgrims and increase his power in the region. The settlers were quite surprised to discover that the Indian who had arrived in their village spoke English.

Samoset later brought Massasoit and 60 warriors to visit the Pilgrims. Dressed in simply fashioned animal skins and moccasins, Massasoit greeted Governor John

Carver and the colonists. When he left, the sachem assigned one of his men to stay as his representative and to aid the struggling settlers in their efforts to survive in a strange land. Hobomok, "a man of account for his valor and parts amongst ye Indians," was chosen to live with the Pilgrims.

The Wampanoags showered the Pilgrims with gifts. Regarding Wampanoag hospitality, Roger Williams wrote that "whomsoever cometh in when they are eating, they offer them to eat of that which they have, though but little enough prepar'd for themselves. If any provision of fish or flesh come in, they make their neighbors partakers with them."

But not all of the colonists were so enthusiastic about the native's helpfulness. Most of the Plymouth residents tried to avoid the Indians while traveling in the woods, and they discouraged the Wampanoags from visiting their

The Wampanoag sachem Massasoit, accompanied by 60 warriors, visited the Pilgrims soon after their arrival at Plymouth. Offering gifts and guidance, the Indians warmly greeted the newcomers to their land.

village as well. As Edward Winslow, who would later become governor of Plymouth, wrote after refusing Massasoit's offer to stay at the village of Sowams:

> We desired to keep the Sabbath at home, and feared we should either be light-headed for want of sleep, for what with bad lodging, the savages' barbarous singing (for they use to sing themselves to sleep), lice and fleas within doors, and mosquitoes without, we could hardly sleep all the time of our being there; we much fearing that if we should stay any longer, we should not be able to recover home for want of strength.

Despite their feelings about the Indians' way of life, the agricultural aid provided by the Indians did not go unrecognized by the settlers. The seeds that the Pilgrims had brought over from England, including wheat and peas, did not germinate that first year. The Indians showed the new settlers how to raise their native corn. In the words of colonist William Wood, they did this "by teaching us to cull out the finest seed, to observe the fittest season, to keep distance for holes and fit measure for hills, to worm it, and weed it, to prune it, and dress it as occasion requires."

With Indian assistance, the Pilgrims' first harvest was so plentiful that a celebratory feast was called for. This feast was appropriately shared with the Indians, for without their help and grains there would have been no harvest to enjoy. Accompanied by 90 of his men, Massasoit arrived at this first Thanksgiving with 5 deer to add to the meal. For three days, the two peoples celebrated the richness of their land.

During the festival, it seemed to both groups that peace was possible and that goodwill could smooth over the difficult relationship between them. When the celebration was over, the sated sachem returned to his homeland, pleased with the results of his help to the colonists.

Massasoit confirmed his loyalty to the English by informing colonist Edward Winslow of rumors that the Massachusett Indians were conspiring against the leaders of Plymouth Colony.

3

PRIDE AND SACRILEGE

Not all of the Indians in the Northeast were interested in maintaining good relations with the new settlers. In the fall of 1621, the powerful Narragansetts sent a hostile message to the Pilgrims—a bundle of arrows wrapped in a snakeskin. But the Pilgrims, with Captain Miles Standish as their military leader, were not intimidated. They sent the skin back loaded down with bullets.

The Narragansetts never did attack. Possibly they chose not to because Squanto—who had become closely allied with the Pilgrims—told the tribe that the settlers had the plague buried in the floor of their blockhouse. Most of the Indians were aware that the diseases that had ravaged the population were somehow connected to the arrival of the colonists. And as far as the Indians knew, the settlers or Squanto could release the plague to attack the Narrangansetts at any time.

For Massasoit, an alliance with the English would provide a connection to a distant nation with vast military power. As sachem, Massasoit's responsibilities included settling disputes within the tribe and representing the Wampanoags in all relations with outsiders. Unlike a monarchy, where the rules of the king were unilaterally set forth and obeyed, sachemship involved keeping the members of the tribe satisfied. The Wampanoags were under no obligation to follow Massasoit; Indian warriors

33

could leave a tribe at any time when they were in disagreement with their leader. In exchange for his promises not to "injure or do hurt" to the English, Massasoit received English backing in all disputes with his neighbors, which made him a very influential man.

Following English military tradition, Miles Standish created an armed camp within the village of Plymouth. He built a blockhouse for defense against hostile Indians. Standish mounted several expeditions to explore the land around Plymouth for possible settlement sites. Although he returned from those tribes unharmed, he always maintained his belief that the Indians were potentially dangerous. The bellicose Standish saw land conflicts with his Indian neighbors as inevitable. And he believed that the use of force and intimidation was necessary in all dealings with them.

For their part, many Indians were very disturbed by the settlers' aggressive military attitude. But that was not all that bothered them. They were equally upset that the

A 19th-century illustration of Miles Standish en route to the town of Wessagusset, accompanied by a group of colonists and a Wampanoag named Hobomok. At Wessagusset, Standish and his men murdered four tribal elders.

colonists stole their precious corn in the winter, when the tribes' own supplies often ran low. Regarding the Wessagusset settlement to the north, William Bradford wrote:

> And after [the settlers] began to come into wants, many sold away their clothes and bed coverings; others (so base were they) became servants to the Indians, and would cut them wood and fetch them water for a capful of corn; others fell to plain stealing, both night and day, from the Indians, of which they grieviously complained.

These and other troubles eventually caused a rift between Massasoit and the colonists. Using his alliance with Plymouth, Squanto had often threatened other Indians and attempted to undermine Massasoit's power. Edward Winslow wrote that Squanto was a man "whose ends were only to make himself great in the eyes of his countrymen, by means of his nearness and favor with us." When Squanto died, a primary cause of tension between Massasoit and the colonists was eliminated.

Sometime later, their relations were further improved when Winslow helped Massasoit recover from a particularly rough, perhaps life-threatening, bout of constipation. Massasoit then told Winslow of a conspiracy being planned by the Massachuset Indian leaders against Plymouth: This alleged conspiracy could well include tribes from Massachusetts Bay to Cape Cod. Massasoit went on to suggest to Winslow that if the Massachuset leaders were killed first, the plot could be averted before it even began.

The Plymouth leaders decided to follow Massasoit's advice. They sent Captain Miles Standish and eight other men, including the Wampanoag Hobomok, to visit Wessagusset, near where the Massachuset leaders resided. When the small force arrived, Standish pretended that he was there to purchase beaver pelts. He was surprised to see that the settlers at Wessagusset mixed openly with the Indians and had no fort or blockhouse.

The following day, Standish planned a series of surprise attacks on the tribal elders. Four Massachusett Indians—including a man named Wituwamet—were invited to a feast in one of the colonists' homes. When the visitors entered, Standish's men sprang out of the shadows of the room and swiftly killed them. Later in the day, three more Indians were murdered in the same manner.

Obtakiest, the Massachusett sachem, attempted to avenge the death of his fellow tribesmen. But his people refused to join him. They had believed their leaders to be invulnerable, so they were terrified by the news of the men's death.

Standish brought Wituwamet's head back to Plymouth and posted it outside the recently completed fort. It served both as a grim warning to all Indians with thoughts of betrayal or disobedience and as a reminder that the English had declared themselves the new masters of the land.

Almost as soon as the men returned, the evidence against the Massachusett leaders began to crumble. Phineas Pratt, a trader at Wessagusset, who had originally supported Massasoit's claims, revealed that the Massachusetts did not have any allies willing to fight with them. They were simply angered that some members of the Wessagusset settlement had pilfered their tribe's corn. In fact, alliances between Indian tribes in southern New England were very rare. Warfare was still mostly a family matter, one of revenge for personal losses. With further investigation, it became clear that Massasoit had used the appearance of a plot to convince the colonists that he was looking after their interests and wanted to reestablish good relations. He had turned the discontent of a neighboring, rival tribe into an opportunity to prove his loyalty. For their part, the colonists, with the encouragement of the militant Standish, had been more than pleased to believe his claims. They felt little remorse over the deaths of the six Massachusett men. As always, the settlers were glad to rid themselves of potentially dangerous natives.

The inherent contradictions between the Puritans' talk of love and their practice of intimidation and murder did not go unnoticed. As the Nemasket sachem, Corbitant, asked of Edward Winslow in 1623:

> If your love be such, and it bring forth such fruits, how cometh it to pass, that when we come to Patuxet, you stand upon your guard, with the mouths of your pieces presented to us?

Winslow thought quickly and replied that for the colonists pointing a gun at someone was an honor. But Corbitant, rightly, found this reasoning hard to believe. Shaking his head, he said that "he liketh not such salutations."

The colonists adapted quickly to their new environment. Each year more crops were planted and more fish were harvested. But these signs of prosperity often created turmoil for the Indians. The English brought livestock—including horses, cows, and pigs—from their homeland and allowed the animals to roam freely. The livestock was continually getting into Indian cornfields and gardens, causing great damage. When the Indians began to kill the trespassing animals, the English ordered the sachems to fence their fields to prevent further conflicts.

Between 1620 and 1640, there was a great wave of European immigration. French settlers landed to the north in regions that would later become known as Quebec and Nova Scotia. The Dutch settled to the south in present-day New York State. More Puritans landed in Massachusetts Bay and founded the towns of Boston, Roxbury, and Cambridge. The majority of the Puritan settlers held a religious conviction that the new land was rightfully theirs. Most either settled wherever they chose

The map contains numerous place names including: Cochecho, the fall, Lamperele R., Niegheehewanck River, the falls, the Bay, qnamscoke, Shitton, Acomenticus, Strawbery Banke, Pafcataque River, the boresheat, Iflands of Shoulds, Pemacooks Sagamore, Mattacomen, Pifcaconouk Sagamore, Amafkeig, pentuckett, Igowam, Merimoek River, Nefick pond, John Sagamore, Horne ponds, Red Sport ponds, Wongguom, Cap Ann, Mufketiquid, Nahum kek, marble Harbor, C. Ann Harbor, Salem, North R., Nahant poynt, Charle towne, pullen poynt, Boston, Mefachusetts Baye, Mudenfx, Shoqua, Roxbury, Dure gt, Dorchestr, Allerton poynt, Charles R., Nepopfett R., Chickatabut Sagamore, Mount wolliston, Conchifetts, Wanataquut River, Sittoate, Greenes Harbor, Cap Codd, Narrogansetts R., new plymouth, New Plymouth Baye, Wests harbor, The great Baye, old plymouth, Pucanokick Sagamore, Narrogansetts Bay, North, West, East, South, Elizabeths Jle

Between 1620 and 1640, huge numbers of European settlers arrived on the shores of what is now the northeastern United States. By 1634, when this map was drawn, competition between colonists and Indians for land in New England had already grown fierce.

or purchased farms and community land from other colonists with complete disregard for Indian claims to the land.

There were, however, a few people within the communities of New England who disagreed with these policies. Perhaps the most potent dissenting voice was that of Roger Williams. He claimed that the colonists were taking an excessive amount of Indian land and violating the natives' rights. This challenge threatened the Puritans' belief that they were the true owners of the land. His views were deemed so dangerous to the new society that the Massachusetts General Court prepared to banish Williams. He escaped to the south and started the settlement of Rhode Island based on religious tolerance.

Despite losing their land, many Indians seemed to be benefiting from trade with the colonists. Massasoit was surrounded by English goods: copper kettles that were lighter than the Indians' handmade ceramic pots, iron hoes that made farming easier, heavy woven blankets, and the all-important British firearms. He was also draped in wampumpeag, strings of wampum—the Indian-crafted beads they and the settlers often used for trading. The use of this currency was encouraged because trading arms to the Indians was seen as increasingly dangerous. "With this wompompeague," wrote Daniel Gookin, "they pay tribute, redeem captives, satisfy of murders and other wrongs, purchase peace with their potent neighbors, as occasion requires; in a word, it answers all occasions with them, as gold and silver doth with us."

But many Indians had little desire to purchase the colonists' goods, except for the guns and lightweight pots. This casual attitude toward material gain was difficult for the struggling Puritans to comprehend. In their culture, the desire to buy and sell goods was very strong, as was the need to obtain objects as a way of establishing social status.

With some exceptions, the Indians saw little point in killing more animals than was necessary or in owning an excess of skins. Indeed, overhunting was considered an affront to the spirits and to the animals themselves, who were believed to harbor their own inner spirits. But the colonists had no such reverence for the animals. They considered deer to be little more than a "great helpe and refreshment" to supplement their agriculture. Even as Puritan ministers denounced the "lust for gain," many settlers saw the Indians' way of life as a slothful existence that wasted precious land.

Late in 1639, Massasoit visited the house of a nearby settler named Brown. The colonists had once again given the sachem much cause for alarm. He had discussed the brutal fighting ways of the English with his counselors at length. Now, he hoped that he could maintain a lasting peace between his tribe and the powerful settlers.

Massasoit's unease stemmed from an event that had occurred about one year earlier. In 1637, the English had met with some resistance from the Pequots of the Connecticut Valley and had virtually annihilated the tribe. This extreme action was said to be in retaliation for the murder of a vulgar old sea captain. The English army marched on the town of Mystic. Intentionally avoiding the Pequot fort where most of the tribe's warriors were housed, they and their Indian allies slaughtered the women and children of the tribe. They then attacked two Pequot forts in one day. After most of the Pequots were killed, those women and children who survived the massacre were either kept as slaves or sent to the West Indies to be sold in slave markets. The Pequots who escaped slaughter and captivity fled to neighboring tribes.

Brutally massacring men, women, and children, the English almost annihilated the entire Pequot tribe in a 1637 military operation.

After the massacre, Massasoit anxiously sought to reestablish strong ties with Plymouth. Towns and churches had been springing up throughout New England, and he made a strong promise to the Plymouth settlers that he would sell no land without their consent. Eager to reinforce the Wampanoag-Plymouth alliance, Massasoit told the settlers gathered at Brown's house that he wanted good relations to be maintained throughout his sachemship and also when his son Wamsutta would represent the tribe.

The Indians who aided the English in the Pequot slaughter soon regretted their actions. Although they were successful in their attack, they quickly turned on the colonists with anger. In retrospect, they saw the horror of the war in which they had participated. In conflicts between Indian tribes in the region, warfare was traditionally based on retaliation for the loss of family members and was executed with quick guerrilla like raids. When revenge was achieved, the feud was over. But the Pequot war had been a ruthless slaughter, killing warriors, women, and children alike.

The colonists at Brown's house accepted Massasoit's wish graciously, happy to have the upper hand in their relations with the Wampanoags. Over the next few years, the colonists praised their brave soldiers for their efforts against the Indians. New England was ebullient. It seemed that with the Pequot massacre and Massasoit's offer of peace, the Puritans were finally in control. According to Massachusetts Bay colonist Edward Johnson, these "were the glorious days of *New England*."

On hearing the news of the English success against the Pequots, Johnson explained that the Indians' sacrilege had led to their destruction. Not part of the "loving counsell" of the Puritans, the Pequots "blasphemed the Lord. . . . [B]y their horrible pride they fitted themselves for destruction."

NEVVES FROM AMERICA;

OR,

A NEW AND EXPERI-
MENTALL DISCOVERIE OF
NEW ENGLAND;

CONTAINING,

A TRVE RELATION OF THEIR
War-like proceedings these two yeares last
past, with a Figure of the Indian Fort,
or Palizado.

Also a discovery of these places, that as yet have very few or no Inhabitants which would yeeld speciall accommodation to such as will Plant there,

Viz.

Queenapoick,
Aggs-wom,
Hudsons River.
Long Island.
Nahanticut.
Martins Vinyard.
Pequet.
Naransett Bay.
Elizabeth Islands,
Puscataway.
Caske with about a hundred Islands, neere to Casko.

By Captaine IOHN UNDERHILL, a Commander
in the Warres there:

LONDON,
Printed by J.D. for Peter Cole, and are to be sold at the signe
of the Glove in Corne-hill neere the
Royall Exchange. 1638.

No. 1405

4

ᐯ ᐯ ᐯ

TO WRONG THEIR
KINGS

Massasoit's young son Metacom grew up in a world
changing at a dizzy pace. The lives of his fellow
tribespeople were in a state of constant flux as they both
accommodated and resisted English ways. Massasoit, ever
willing to compromise and maintain good relations with
the English, had amassed great power and wealth. As a
result of this alliance, Metacom lived a life of relative
ease and material comfort. But in the eyes of the English
colonists, young Indians were spoiled with affection and
leniency. The results, remarked one English observer,
were "sawcie, bold, and undutifull" children.

In fact, Metacom's older brother, Wamsutta, did
receive special attention. As Massasoit's eldest son, Wamsutta was next in line to become sachem of the Wampanoags after his father's death.

Although he was still in good health, the elderly
sachem suffered under the pressure of his relationship
with the Plymouth settlers. When colonists at Providence
offered to buy a piece of land from him, Massasoit broke
his promise and sold it to the more liberal colony. To
further complicate matters, the land was also claimed by
the Narragansetts. Moreover, the Wampanoag sachem
had lost an important ally when Roger Williams was

The title page from
Underhill's News from
America, *published in 1638.*
Although it touts the "dis-
covery" of farmlands that
"have very few or no In-
habitants," the areas it names
had been occupied by Indians
for centuries.

forced to abandon the Wampanoags in 1636 and settle west of the Taunton River. Williams had been asked by Plymouth, under pressure from the Massachusetts Bay Colony, to leave the lands claimed by the Plymouth colonists. His new settlement was on land that was then controlled by the Narragansetts.

At that time, the Narragansetts were a very strong tribe, with an excess of wampum and powerful leaders. Because they had yet to suffer much from European diseases, their healers, known as *powwows*, were considered to be very powerful. The Narragansett sachems welcomed Williams to their land as a new ally and gave him property to begin Providence Plantation.

Officials at Plymouth were well aware of Massasoit's respect for the banished Williams, who was sympathetic to Indian causes. They pressed the sachem to keep his promise and protect their claim to the land. However, without a royal charter from England, the Plymouth colonists were on shaky ground. Their alleged ownership of the land surrounding their colony, and indeed the colony itself, was almost entirely dependent on treaties with the Wampanoags. If they lost their control over Massasoit, they could well lose all of their land.

As Metacom grew up, the great wave of colonial immigration began to subside. Fewer new settlers arrived, and those who were already there raised children and began to form permanent bonds to the land. In the minds of the colonists, the Indians' relatively simple way of life amounted to a waste of the Lord's land. The settlers used their reasoning to justify taking the land for themselves. As the Indian population dwindled, the colonists quickly moved into their abandoned villages and fields.

The tribes who suffered most from disease also began to lose confidence in the healing powers of their pow-wows. As death approached, some Indians questioned

After clergyman Roger Williams was banished from Plymouth in 1636, he traveled to Narragansett territory, where he was welcomed by the tribe's sachems.

their spiritual beliefs and converted to Christianity. They begged and promised that if the English god would make them well, they would serve him for the rest of their lives. The Wampanoags of Martha's Vineyard, a small island off the coast of present-day Massachusetts, believed that Christian Indians lived longer lives.

In this way, the Puritans' religious zeal was extended to the Indians. Although many Indians had little difficulty accepting an English god, they were not so eager to abandon Cautantowwit. To the Algonkians, life and religion were inseparable. One day in the week was not set aside for religion, as was the Pilgrims' way. But rather, when food was plentiful, the Indians held a celebration to thank the spirits and Cautantowwit. The hunt itself was a spiritual pursuit for the Indians. Everything in the world was believed to be within the gods' realm, and the Indians trusted that the gods would provide for them.

Massasoit, who freely sold lands to and signed treaties with Plymouth colonists, refused to bow to Puritan pressure to convert. He pleaded with the Plymouth authorities not to "draw any of his People from their old *Pagan Superstition.*" According to 20th-century historian T. H. Breen, very few Native Americans had any desire "to live in stuffy cabins, attend white schools, give up traditional religious practices, copy English government, adopt European medicines, or, much to the colonist's amazement, make love to white women." On the other hand, and perhaps more shocking to the colonists, there were a number of whites, who, after being captured during battles with Indians, adapted to the natives' way of life. Once accustomed to the Indian ways, these captives often showed little desire to return to their colonies and, in some cases, actually had to be forced to leave their new Indian community by their captors.

Unlike the Indians, who considered religion a more personal matter, the Puritans were inflexible. The church was the center of their life. The Puritans regarded the Indians as a force outside the all-important realm of the Lord. In their mind, anything beyond the warmth of God's hearth was in the spiritual darkness of the devil.

The difference in skin color further enhanced the colonists' prejudice against the Indians. Although the early colonists did not make overt references to the Indians' skin color as red, they never allowed Native Americans to become more than second-class citizens while living in their towns. During this time of prosperity for both groups, Metacom could walk the streets of Boston or Plymouth, proudly displaying his wealth, but he could never be accepted into colonial society.

Within that society, Puritanism was the essential common element. The newly formed United Colonies of New England, consisting of Connecticut, Massachusetts Bay, New Haven, and Plymouth, was established in 1643 with this crucial religious conviction as its foundation. As non-Puritans, the inhabitants of Rhode Island and Native Americans were excluded from the alliance.

The first actions taken by the United Colonies were designed to control and intimidate insubordinate Indians. They joined forces against the Narragansett sachem, Miantonomi, who dared to challenge both their requests for land and their demands for subjugation. Rhode Island joined forces with the Narragansetts. The United Colonies ordered Uncas of the Mohegan tribe to assassinate Miantonomi. After he was killed, Ninigret of the Niantic Indians took the brunt of the United Colonies' grievances.

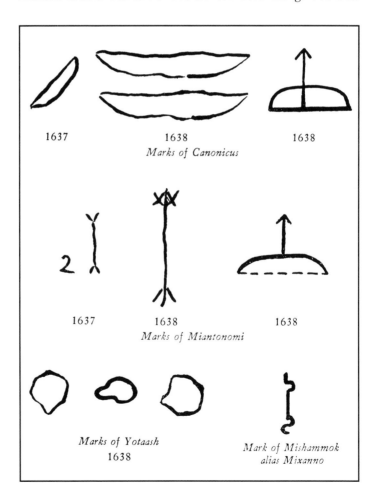

1637   1638   1638
Marks of Canonicus

1637   1638   1638
Marks of Miantonomi

Marks of Yotaash
1638

*Mark of Mishammok
alias Mixanno*

The marks used by four Narragansett sachems to sign official documents.

According to England's mandate for settlers, one of the goals of the new colonies was to "incite the Natives of [the] Country to the knowledge and obedience of the onlie true God and Savior of Mankinde." At first, the Massachusetts Bay Colony had little interest in converting the Indians to their faith. But as pressure and protests from England began to affect the economy of the colony, plans were made to build missions.

Converting the Indians, at least at Massachusetts Bay, involved much more than convincing them to accept the Puritan god. Missionary John Eliot, known as "the apostle" to the Indians, tried to create missions that resembled English settlements. Not only was prayer or worship of Cautantowwit forbidden, but native converts were expected to cut their hair and work hard at making baskets, brooms, and pots for the colonists. Instead of sharing surpluses of venison, berries, or fish with others, the Indians were taught to sell their excess food. Habits that the Puritans deemed filthy—such as killing body lice by breaking them between the teeth—were heartily discouraged. Perhaps most important, converted Indians were required to obey all the laws of Massachusetts Bay. Before the Indians could become practicing Christians, they were expected to discontinue observing their native customs and completely sever all ties to their tribe.

After 25 years of missionary work, fewer than 100 Indians received communion at the Boston settlement. Hugh Peter, who succeeded Roger Williams as pastor of Salem and later excommunicated him, admitted that the work at these missions "was but a plain cheat, and that there was no such thing as a gospel conversion among the Indians."

There were other missions, such as the one at Martha's Vineyard, that were less stringent and had more converts during these years. Many of the Indians who accepted

Missionary John Eliot tried to convert the Wampanoags not only to Christianity but also to the colonists' way of life.

the settlers' religious beliefs came to regard those Indians who resisted the new way as being in league with the devil. Conversely, the Indians who maintained their traditional way of life were extremely suspicious of the Christain Indians. Metacom later related his own views on religion to colonist John Easton:

> [The sachems] had a great fear to have any of their Indians . . . called or forced to be Christian Indians. They said that such were in everything more Mischievous, only Dissemblers, and [that] the English made them not subject to their Kings, and by their lying to wrong their Kings.

But it was not only the mission Indians who were subject to the new system of laws established by the United Colonies. The English system of justice became increasingly unjust for all Indians. It was tremendously difficult for Indians to bring their cases to court. Naturally, they had many complaints against their English neighbors, but the colonial magistrates were not eager to hear their lengthy claims.

Among their tribespeople, Indians told stories with relish, using grand gestures and pausing often for dramatic effect. An interested audience listened in silence, smoking and nodding. The colonists and their magistrates, however, were not held in such rapt attention by the detailed accounts of their own wrongdoings. Eventually all Indians were banned from entering Plymouth on the day of court hearings. The Indians were only allowed to present their cases in July and October, and with the large number of complaints, there was never time to hear them all.

As the English enjoyed increasing wealth and prosperity, the Wampanoags became increasingly alarmed. Their land and their game continued to diminish, leaving them with less to trade and therefore less power in their dealings with the colonists. The Wampanoag men—most of whom no longer hunted solely for food—shot or trapped beavers for the goods that the animals' pelts would bring from the English. But the colonists' thirst for beaver pelts had ground to a halt.

Now the strong snares that the Indians set in autumn to trap deer were almost always empty. Beavers were becoming scarce, and in general the quantities of game the colonists had observed when they first arrived had vanished. Along with the gradual disappearance of the beaver and white-tailed deer, the elk, bear, and lynx were virtually eradicated as the 17th century progressed. With their own domestic animals on which to feed, the colonists had little need of the Indians' game for meat. Indian sachems had only the land left to offer. And the Indians with less power could offer only cheap labor.

The settlers, who had never relied heavily on hunting, adapted easily to the changes in the environment. Their cattle, sheep, corn, and peas were thriving. A few unusually warm winters also helped the colonists. Some believed that their clearing of the land had been responsible for the favorable weather. Virtually all were convinced that it was Christ's will that they tame the land.

As spiritually advantageous as clearing of the land was for the colonists, it was both economically and spiritually damaging to the Indians. The act of hunting furs for trade had already created a spiritual crisis. The Algonkians believed that each animal had an individual spirit that should be honored and respected. Encouraged by the colonists, they had exchanged these honorable beings for goods and supplies. Those Indians who had not been converted to Christianity (the vast majority) could easily see why the gods were angry with their tribes and why the animals themselves had disappeared.

As the price of beaver pelts declined, so did the value of wampum against the English shilling. In the early 1660s, the value of wampum became so low that Plymouth pronounced that it was no longer a legal currency. Although the English attempted to explain to the Indians that this was a result of changing markets in England, the Indians, unaccustomed to such shifts, could only see it as a an attempt by the settlers to cheat them. They watched as the English prospered on the lands that had once been theirs, whereas they themselves suffered more each year.

Metacom was hardly bothered by these problems while growing up at Montaup. Although he was a "prince" in the eyes of the colonists, he lived the life of any young Wampanoag. He spent his time canoeing in the bay and along the river and walking along the beach with his brother. Metacom heard the complaints his father had lodged against the colonists, and he often listened to the grievances of his counselors, but it was his brother who would inherit these problems and the responsibility for solving them.

Nonetheless, the problems existed. During Metacom's childhood the use of alcohol was common among his tribe. Soon this too complicated the Indians' lives. Alcohol abuse became rampant and soon disrupted the lives of all tribespeople. Although the sachems reportedly drank in moderation, Daniel Gookin wrote that "many of the Indians were great lovers of strong drink, [such] as aqua vitae, rum, brandy, or the like, and are very greedy to buy it of the English." Selling liquor to Indians was illegal in Massachusetts Bay, but many colonists were eager to profit from black-market sales.

Some of the Wampanoags maintained an almost perpetual state of drunkenness. This not only made them boisterous nuisances to their neighbors but also severely compromised their ability to act as warriors. Metacom

A wampum belt that was possibly owned by Metacom. Shell beads known as wampum were a popular form of currency used in trading between the Indians and the colonists.

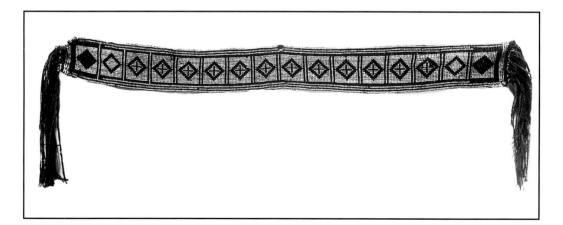

later complained to John Easton that the Indian sachems, "Sum being given to drunknes," were plied with alcohol by colonial officials, only to be cheated after "the English made them drunk." Metacom's anger grew after many years of listening to Massasoit and his counselors discuss the tricks English traders used on the Indians. Then he saw these same Indian leaders left with scarcely any land as a result of these devious strategies.

Still, as long as Massasoit was willing to work to maintain relations with the colonists, there would be no serious threat of violence. Defying some of his counselors, who warned him that the English might become too powerful if they were not stopped, Massasoit continued to believe it was possible to get protection and wealth from his English neighbors. For most of his life, he sought a peaceful coexistence with the colonists. But as the next generation grew up, the balance between the two groups was becoming increasingly tense.

5

"KING" OF THE WAMPANOAGS

In early 1660, when Massasoit was about 80 years old, the sachem died. Indian leaders and some colonists from Plymouth arrived for his burial. Aged men themselves, the colonists looked on the passing of an important friend and ally with sadness.

After mourning Massasoit's death, the young Wamsutta became the focus of many celebrations held to mark his rise to the rank of sachem. Indian ambassadors from tribes throughout the region were sent to join in the festivities honoring the new leader.

But not all of New England was celebrating. As the news of Massasoit's death spread, many of the Plymouth colonists grew anxious. They wondered if the young sachem would respect the treaties they had negotiated with Massasoit. Although Massasoit may have been indifferent at times, he rarely displayed anger or disobeyed the wishes of the Plymouth General Court. The members of the court could not be so sure that Wamsutta would be so easily controlled.

Within the year, Wamsutta and his younger brother Metacom traveled to Plymouth with a group of Wampanoag men. It was the first official meeting between the proud new chief and the Plymouth colonists.

A 19th-century engraving of Philip, who was dubbed King by the English when he became the Wampanoag sachem.

55

Arriving at the Plymouth General Court, Wamsutta announced his and his brother's intention to adopt English names as an act of respect for the colonists. For the Wampanoags, names held supernatural power and were highly guarded, so much so that it was considered rude to refer to a person by his or her true name. The taking of a new name indicated the birth of a new person.

The members of the court, perhaps somewhat mockingly, decided to give the two Indians names from classical history. Wamsutta was called Alexander, possibly after Alexander the Great, the Macedonian king who conquered Greece in about 300 B.C. Metacom became known as Philip, the name of Alexander the Great's father.

Alexander's appearance at the court was not enough to ease the tension between the Indians and the colonists. The new sachem freely sold land—both his own and that of the Pocasset sachem Weetamoo—to neighboring colonists without Plymouth's consent. Although tribal lands were dwindling, the sales were necessary to obtain arms and other colonial goods. Dependent on Wampanoag land, the colonists at Plymouth grew more and more discontented by the news of these sales.

And the lust for more land was becoming rampant among the colonists. Initially, the Pilgrims were attracted to the idea of communal living. But their interest in sharing the land was lost once they realized that private land ownership gave them more opportunities for private gain. Puritan clergyman Increase Mather wrote that the settlers, who had previously been content with small plots of land, now "coveted after the earth, [so] that many hundreds, nay thousands of Acres, have been engrossed by one man." But such complaints were rare. As the dangerous frontier receded, the colonists failed to consider the ethics of seizing more and more territory.

Soon after establishing their first villages in North America, the English colonists' desire for more land began to appear insatiable, greatly alarming their Indian neighbors.

In 1662, Alexander refused to travel to Plymouth to confirm his loyalty to the General Court. Provoked by this slight, the colonists felt that the time had come to teach him who was actually in control of the land. The court sent a representative to speak with Alexander.

The sachem received the message from Plymouth gracefully. But it did not convince him to stop selling land. Like his father, Alexander considered Roger Williams and his fellow colonists to be more honest and peaceful traders. So, despite Plymouth's objections, he proceeded to make more deals with the Rhode Island colonists.

The Plymouth colonists decided that they could no longer endure Alexander's disregard for their authority. Officials of the General Court decided that a more forceful "talk" with the young sachem was in order. This time, they dispatched a small military force under the command of Major Josiah Winslow to bring Alexander to Plymouth by whatever means necessary.

Winslow and his men approached the Indian camp carefully, catching Alexander and his men off guard. The major immediately drew his gun and pointed it at Alexander's breast. Although Alexander was ill, he had no choice but to leave with the armed Winslow. Along with a few aides and his sons, the ailing sachem, marching while Winslow rode on his steed, headed down the road to Plymouth.

The long walk took a heavy toll upon Alexander. At Plymouth, he was vigorously questioned by the new governor, Thomas Prence. When the colonists realized that Alexander was indeed very ill, he was released. But the Plymouth authorities insisted that he leave his two sons as hostages.

The decision to release the sachem came too late, however. Alexander was carried by his men most of the way home. But before he reached the village, his illness overtook him. Halfway between Plymouth and Mount Hope, Alexander died beside the Taunton River on June 8, 1662.

Although it appeared to some of the warriors that Alexander had died of natural causes, others blamed the hard-heartedness of the Plymouth authorities for the sachem's death. Still others believed that Winslow and his armed men had poisoned the sachem and then left him to die. But even those who doubted the use of poison were disturbed by Winslow's brutal behavior toward their sachem. Winslow and his men had not treated the Wampanoag leader with due respect—especially considering his condition. Instead, they treated Alexander as they would a common criminal. Most of the Wampanoags agreed that the colonists were responsible for the sachem's death.

Josiah Winslow, governor of Plymouth Colony between 1673 and 1681.

Philip, now in his mid-twenties, found himself the leader of the disgruntled Wampanoags. After a mourning ritual for Alexander was enacted, ceremonies to honor the new chief began. Long nights of dancing and feasting followed. Ambassadors and leaders from tribes throughout the region came to recognize the new sachem.

When the ceremonies were over, the ambassadors and Philip's counselors met to discuss their views of the colonists. Some undoubtedly felt that after the death of Alexander it was finally time to take up arms against the rapacious English. Others still believed peace was the only alternative, arguing that the colonists' superior weapons and ever-increasing numbers gave them an overwhelming advantage over the Indians.

Philip found himself in a predicament that few sachems before him could have imagined but that many Indian leaders across the continent would later share. He could allow the English to continue taking Wampanoag land by selling off large parcels as they were demanded. Or he could sell only select portions of land and thus retain a measure of autonomy for his people. Either way, his people risked a great loss. They might lose their wealth and heritage if he continued to sell the land. Or they could face virtual extinction, as the Pequots had decades earlier.

On August 6, 1662, the Plymouth colonists summoned Philip to the General Court. The court announced its intention to oversee all land sales made by Philip and his people. The colonists, taking advantage of Philip's inability to read English, told him that the treaty he was signing was valid for seven years. If he held to his bargain, he would encounter no trouble with Plymouth during that time. Unknowingly, Philip signed a document that gave Plymouth control over the sale of Wampanoag land forever. Whenever Philip mentioned his seven-year obligation, the colonists never corrected him.

In 1667, the Plymouth General Court reneged on its promise to prevent settlement on Indian lands and established the town of Swansea near the Wampanoags' homeland at Sowams. Settlers moved in, erected houses and a church, and began tilling the land. Forests were cleared for more pastures and fields.

The town's proximity to Indian land was a threat to the traditional pursuits of the Wampanoags. Indian hunters were jailed by the court for "trespassing" on English lands. This concept of exclusive ownership was difficult for the Indians to understand. They were accustomed to sharing the wealth of the land among themselves.

Philip held true to the treaty for seven years. In 1671, believing he was free to sell as much land as he wished to whomever he pleased, he once again began to discuss land sales with the Rhode Island colonists. At the same time, rumors of Wampanoag war preparations were making the officials anxious. The Plymouth colonists called Philip to court and accused him of conspiring with the Narragansetts to reclaim their native lands by waging war.

Philip, noting the Plymouth court's eagerness to keep him in line, began to question his father's practice of appeasing the colonists. Philip had a strong resolve to protect the interests of his people, and he was less inclined to be as diplomatic and scheming as his father had been. In hindsight, Massasoit's alliance with the English seemed to have done little more than make the Wampanoags slaves of the English and perhaps add a few wampum beads to his coat.

Fear of the "savages" was on the rise. The English outlawed the sale of guns to the Indians. Philip had to turn to the black market, through which he could buy weapons without the knowledge of the court. The young sachem began to trust his father's subservient ways less and less. Making his own plans for the future, Philip began to heed more closely the words of a former Narragansett sachem:

> For so we are all Indians . . . and say brother to one
> another; so we must be one as [the English] are, otherwise
> we shall all be gone shortly.

6

ENGLISH TROUBLE

The troubled sachem awoke at dawn to the songs of sparrows in the trees. He surveyed the Wampanoag land from the crest of Mount Hope. There were now more cattle than deer in the area surrounding his home. As Swansea expanded, Plymouth's promise of no English trouble seemed to be an an empty one.

The tribespeople awaited Philip's decision. Young warriors, eager to take a stand, were afraid that their sachem had begun to act like a puppet of the English. The colonists had taken their land and changed, perhaps irreparably, the life of the tribe. If these warriors had their way, the tribe would attack the settlers or at least ravage some of their land. In early 1671, Philip allowed his warriors to display their arms in front of Swansea as a warning against further expansion into Wampanoag lands.

Plymouth reacted quickly to this sign of aggression. On April 10, 1671, Philip was called to Taunton to account for the actions of his men in front of representatives from Plymouth and the United Colonies. The well-armed colonists ordered Philip to hand over all of the tribe's weapons. Surrounded by English soldiers, Philip had no alternative but to agree. He relinquished 70 weapons to the colonists as a token of his willingness to comply. This act struck a blow to Philip's power as sachem. His men

As hostilities grew between Plymouth leaders and King Philip, Canonchet — the sachem of the wealthy and powerful Narragansetts — declared that his people would remain neutral.

could not defend themselves properly without arms. Perhaps more importantly, the Indians depended on their weapons for hunting and for their prestige. Even as he made the promise, Philip knew he would not keep it. As sachem, he did not have the right to disarm Wampanoag warriors. Perhaps, as he surrendered his arms to the colonists, Philip planned to unite other tribes against the English. Nevertheless, although he agreed to comply with Plymouth's wishes, Philip made one stipulation: Massachusetts Bay would mediate between the two groups should further problems arise. Years ago, he had visited Boston and been treated very well there. He trusted the Bay colonists and believed that they would help him should he be betrayed.

In the months that followed, the Wampanoags delivered no more guns to the colonists. Philip had known the warriors would never agree to make themselves completely vulnerable either to the colonists or to nearby tribes, such as the Narragansetts. Contact between the Wampanoags and Plymouth during this period was sporadic. Soon rumors spread from the frontier villages that the Wampanoags were preparing for war. When they reached Plymouth, a representative was once again sent to summon Philip to court.

James Brown arrived at Mount Hope and gave Philip the order. Angered by the audacity of Plymouth's demands, the sachem traveled to Massachusetts Bay instead. There, he appealed Plymouth's inappropriate treatment of his people. Although the Bay officials were conciliatory, they told Philip that all decisions must ultimately be made by Plymouth.

Frustrated, Philip refused any further dealings with the governor's ambassador or with the governor himself. Insulted by the treatment he had received, he boldly called for the respect befitting a sachem. Because the governor was only a subject to the king, he demanded a meeting with King Charles himself. This idea was rejected by the colonists as preposterous.

On September 29, 1671, Philip again appeared at Plymouth General Court. Even tighter restrictions were imposed, and Philip formally relinquished his power to the court. From that day forward, he and his people would be subject to all of Plymouth's laws. And as punishment for breaking his earlier agreements, Philip was ordered to pay a fine of 100 British pounds. Again, Nathaniel Morton, secretary of the General Court, did not bother to record the tactics used to force Philip to sign another treaty, which virtually destroyed his tribe's identity as an autonomous nation.

Back at Mount Hope, Philip was accused of cowardice by his own people. He argued with his counselors that he had never planned to comply with the agreement's impossible demands. The possibility of waging war was then seriously discussed by Philip and his counselors for the first time. Over the next three years, the resentment between the Wampanoags and the Plymouth colonists continued to grow. During these tense years, the bonds that had developed between the two societies were, for the most part, dissolved. Neither Philip nor Josiah Winslow, then Plymouth's governor, made any attempt to reconcile their differences until it was too late.

In December 1674, after three years of general discontentment among the Wampanoags, Christian Indian John Sassamon arrived at Plymouth. He came to warn the officials that Philip was planning to attack Swansea. In January, the informer was found with a broken neck in a frozen pond near his home. Winslow decided to use Sassamon's death as a way to take action against Philip.

A few months after Sassamon's body was discovered, three of Philip's men were executed for the murder after

a show trial at the Plymouth General Court. It was the first time Plymouth officials had executed an Indian for a crime that did not involve a colonist. In the past, theft or murder among the Indians had been considered tribal matters to be dealt with by the sachem and his counselors. To Philip's warriors, the executions were outright murder. According to the warriors, the primary witness was an Indian who owed a gambling debt to one of the accused men, so his testimony was clearly prejudiced. There was little real evidence against the men. Betrayed and angry, Philip felt he had every reason to complain.

When Philip arrived in Plymouth to demand retribution for the unjust executions, the court instead questioned him as to his involvement in the affair. He insisted that he had nothing to do with Sassamon's death. The English could produce no proof against the furious

An engraving from the 19th century of the discovery of Christian Indian John Sassamon's body. The Plymouth General Court found three of Philip's men guilty of Sassamon's murder, although little real evidence against them was presented at their trial.

sachem, so he was released. Philip left the colony more enraged than ever.

It is difficult to assess whether Philip did in fact call for Sassamon's death or whether the men who were executed were actually guilty. Sassamon had been an informer for Plymouth on other occasions, as well as an aide to both Philip and Alexander. (Philip had dismissed Sassamon from his court after Sassamon was caught usurping land for himself and his heirs in a transaction between Philip and the colonists.) Either way, after the executions, preparations for war began on both sides.

Aware of the growing tensions, the Massachusetts Bay Colony, in its role as mediator, sent out small parties of men to quell the uprising. One group spoke with leaders from a neighboring tribe, the Nipmucks, and convinced them to pledge allegiance to the English. A commission met with the Narragansett leaders at their headquarters and received a cold response to their threats of retaliation should the Narragansetts side with Philip. The colonists left feeling both confident that the Narragansetts had not yet cast their lot with the Wampanoags and nervous about the future. The most important group of mediators, sent to meet with Philip, arrived too late.

In the summer of 1675, the leading Wampanoag warriors gathered with Philip at his home in Mount Hope and began a two-week war dance. Philip knew that his men could not defeat the Plymouth colonists—with their superior firepower and strategic positions—without the support of other tribes. As the war drums sounded over Mount Hope, he imagined a grand Indian alliance, a united force made up of the Wampanoags, the mighty Narragansetts to the east, and the vast Nipmuck nation to the north.

Young, aggressive Wampanoag warriors began to make raids on settlers' farms. At first, the raids were not violent, but it became clear that it would soon be impossible to quell the Indians' outrage. If Philip could not govern to their satisfaction, they would no longer recognize him as sachem. Unable to yield any further to Plymouth's expansion, Philip decided it was time to take a stand.

One man did try to stop the ensuing bloodbath. John Easton, now the deputy governor of Rhode Island, went to visit Philip. Although there had been many rumors of war since the signing of the Taunton treaty, Easton suspected that this time the Indians were serious. As a Quaker, the deputy governor believed in nonviolence. He hoped to settle the differences between the two groups through mediation. Accompanied by 40 of his men, Philip met with Easton in one last attempt at negotiation. Still awaiting word from the officials at Plymouth, the indignant sachem unleashed a torrent of complaints. In Easton, he finally found a listener who did not flatly refute all of his claims. In a speech made that day, the sachem explained:

> The English who came first to this country were but a handful of people, forlorn, poor and distressed. My father was then sachem, he relieved their distresses in the most kind and hospitable manner. He gave them land to plant and build upon. . . . [They] flourished and increased. By various means they got possession of a great part of his territory. But he still remained their friend till he died. My elder brother became sachem. . . . He was seized and confined and thereby thrown into illness and died. Soon after I became sachem they disarmed my people . . . [and] their land was taken. But a small part of the dominion of my ancestors remains. I am determined not to live until I have no country.

Easton argued that any armed resistance undertaken by the Wampanoags would be unsuccessful because the English were now much more powerful. To this statement, one of the Indians replied that the English should

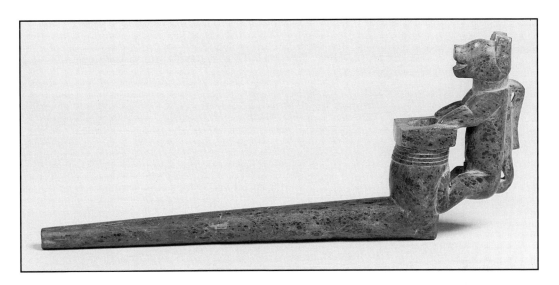

A steatite tobacco pipe that is believed to have belonged to Philip.

treat them as the Indians had treated the English when *they* were vulnerable. Easton recorded that Philip was determined to confront the land issues that had been a source of conflict for so many years. And apparently Philip considered Easton's proposal that he continue to look for a peaceful solution. On June 17, he ordered his warriors to return the horses they had stolen from the settlers.

But Plymouth had no interest in Philip's decisive words or in his attempts at peace. Settlers across the region waited anxiously for the news of the Indian rebellion. A few days later, Easton received a letter from Plymouth declaring a state of emergency in the colony. All negotiations with Philip were off.

Having received no hopeful words from Easton, the frustrated sachem could no longer detain his men. Wampanoag raids on Swansea led to bloodshed, and Plymouth armed forces were dispatched to Swansea and Mount Hope.

As the Plymouth colonists struggled to decide how best to fight Philip, the alliances that they assumed existed between the Wampanoags and other tribes were far from a reality. When the Indians heard of the spreading war, most of the tribes could not decide which side to support.

Among the Narragansetts, one of the strongest tribes, there was no disagreement. When the first blood was spilled by Philip's warriors, the Narragansetts were quick to explain to the colonists that they were not eager to fight the English. But the times when the wealthy and powerful Narragansetts could remain indifferent to the struggles between the colonists and the smaller tribes had long past. Since the decimation of the Pequots, the Narragansett sachem, Canonchet, had seen that some involvement in politics and diplomacy was necessary. Still, for the time being, the powerful tribe chose to remain neutral.

Assawompsett Pond in Massachusetts, photographed in 1919 from the location of Philip's lookout during the war.

Plymouth's motives for refusing to negotiate were revealed in a letter written later that year from a Boston merchant to the London Gazette, a newspaper published in England. The letter claimed that Philip's tribe had been removed from the Mount Hope peninsula. It also estimated the value of the land to be 10,000 pounds sterling. This was a considerable sum for any colony, but especially for Plymouth. The Massachussetts Bay Colony had grown larger by annexing present-day Maine and vast areas to the north, but Plymouth had little room left to expand. The Wampanoag land would be a great boon to their colony.

The report also warned that if the land was taken by force it might cause increased hostility among the tribes. The colonists assumed that Philip was gathering forces among neighboring Indians, urging them to put aside their past squirmishes, for "if [the Indians] did not Joyn together, they should lose their lives and their lands."

7

"DEVILS IN DESPERATION"

Although there was no united Indian force preparing to attack the frontier towns, as many colonists feared, most of the Wampanoags were ready to follow Philip into battle. The powerful Pocasset sachem, Weetamoo, Philip's sister-in-law, was one of his first allies. Weetamoo had foreseen conflicts developing over the diminishing Indian lands even before Philip did. She had protested when Alexander sold her own tribal lands, which lay to the east of the Wampanoag territory. Her complaints were acknowledged by the Plymouth General Court and the sales were stopped. Mary Rowlandson, a settler who was at one time held as a slave by the Pocasset sachem, wrote of Weetamoo:

> A severe and proud Dame she was, bestowing every Day in dressing herself near as much Time as any of the Gentry of the Land: Powdering her Hair and painting her Face, going with her Necklaces, with Jewels in her Ears, and Bracelets upon her hands.

When Philip's tribe fled from Mount Hope and took refuge at Weetamoo's village, the Pocasset men were eager to join with their Indian neighbors. The warriors covered their skin and hair with swine fat to protect them from insects and sunburn. In fact, the Indians hated the English pigs, and they killed them with relish for their

73

fat. Of all the English livestock, it was those free-roaming "filthy cut throats," as the Indians referred to the pigs, that had done the most damage to their crops over the years. Despite the warriors' excitement, Philip anticipated the impending conflict with anxiety, because he had no way of knowing the size of the colonial army gathering at his former headquarters.

The Plymouth colonists were just completing their fort at Mount Hope when a Massachusetts Bay Colony force of about 200 soldiers left to confront the Narragansetts. Benjamin Church, one of the men in the Plymouth army, was particularly eager to destroy Philip. He wanted to be sure that they reached him before he could gather allies. Church crossed Mount Hope Bay with about 40 men, but when they were confronted by the well-armed Indians, the colonists froze in terror. Church tried to lead the men into the depths of the swamp, where the Indians were hiding in the thick brush, but the weight of their muskets and their fear prevented the colonists from proceeding. Church held his ground at the edge of the river until his party was rescued by a passing boat.

While the Massachusetts army was holding off the Narragansetts, in an attempt to prevent them from entering the war on the side of the Wampanoags, native forces led by Philip began to strike. Middleborough—a small settlement in the Plymouth colony close to where Sassamon's body had been found months earlier—was attacked first. Then the settlements at Rehoboth, Swansea, and Taunton were hit, and the colonists' cattle were stolen. At Dartmouth, settlers were murdered, then disemboweled. More than two dozen houses were razed to the ground. In all likelihood, Philip spent much of this time in the Pocasset swamp. But many historians credit him with planning the outbreaks of violence that exploded throughout the region.

Benjamin Church, a member of the Plymouth army and an important chronicler of King Philip's War.

A combined force of colonists, mostly from Connecticut, and about 40 Mohegan Indians gathered on August 1. They were met by a contingent of Wampanoags north of Providence. The colonial forces killed about 50 Wampanoags, but Philip held off the settlers. Although the skirmish was considered a victory by the colonists, such small achievements did little to prevent the aggression building within the Indian tribes. By failing to mount a full-scale offensive, the colonists allowed Philip the opportunity to flee north and recruit even more allies.

By this time Philip's forces were well armed with muskets and gunpowder, but as he was traveling with women and children, he could not risk a major battle with the colonial forces. The warriors, who had held off the invaders near Providence, retreated into the swamps. From there they planned to flee north into Nipmuck country. Fighting at Philip's side was Annawon, Philip's chief officer and one of his closest friends.

It was decided that the women and children would take refuge with the neutral Narragansetts. Although sachem Canonchet and the other Narragansetts were reluctant to accept the nonfighting Wampanoags at first, they were eventually accepted into the safety of the tribe.

After taking leave of his wife and son, Philip was constantly on the move. The Indians' quick attacks kept the English on the defensive. The English were surprisingly short of arms and provisions. As soon as the war broke out, James Cudworth, the leader of Plymouth's forces at Mount Hope, wrote Governor Winslow requesting more ammunition in preparation for Indian attacks. Governor Winslow replied that he had no ammunition to spare.

The settlers also lost energy, having to rely on inadequate food supplies while searching for Philip in the swamps and forests. The Indians fared better, being more accustomed to minimal food rations. They were capable of making a good dinner from, in Roger Williams's words, "a *spoonfull* of [parched] *meale* and a spoonfull of water from the *Brooke*." They also had a greater knowledge of the edible roots, fruits, and seeds available in the woods and boggy areas.

As the colonists marched through the swamps, they were unnerved by the abundance of rattlesnakes. The Indians' ability to hide in the bushes and marsh grass also kept the colonists on edge. Soldiers would frequently shoot at any nearby motion, wasting precious ammunition. Sometimes their jittery nerves cost them more than mere powder and bullets. As Increase Mather wrote: "Our Men when in that hideous Place, if they did but see a Bush stir, would fire presently, whereby it is verily feared they did sometimes unhappily shoot English Men instead of Indians."

Benjamin Church found the slow pace of his fellow soldiers very frustrating. He complained about the "epidemical plague of lust after Tobacco," knowing that every time the soldiers stopped to smoke and relax, the Indians gained ground in front of them.

Although the war was not an organized drive to push the white settlers back into the sea, as colonial historians often portrayed it, Philip's battle did offer an outlet for the hostility and resentment that had long been harbored among other tribes. The Nipmuck mission Indians rose against their oppressors almost as soon as they heard the rumors of war. Philip's cousin Awashonks, the sachem of the Sakonnets, joined the conflict after the Rhode Island colonists, who had promised to protect her, allowed her tribe to be attacked by Plymouth forces. Even without time to organize, the colonists' racist fears and aggressive tactics brought Philip allies from all over New England.

The Nipmucks were a mighty tribe and traditional allies of the Wampanoags even before Massasoit's sachemship. As he traveled through the Nipmuck villages, Philip convinced most of the population to join with him. About 3,000 Nipmucks were scattered over hundreds of square miles. Their first act of allegiance to Philip was to kill an English captain named Edward Hutchinson and some of his men outside Brookfield, Massachusetts. The *London Gazette* in January 1676 reported that the captain was killed 40 years to the day after his mother, Anne Hutchinson, a famous religious reformer who had been banished from Boston, had been murdered by Indians. The successful Nipmuck warriors went on to besiege and burn much of Brookfield later that day.

The Nipmucks accepted their Wampanoag brothers, even though some of the Nipmucks had once been armed by the colonists with guns and charged to "teach [the other Nipmucks] the fear of the Lord." Nipmuck warriors rose up and torched the nearby towns. Beginning in September, Mendon, Hadley, Hatfield, and Northampton were ambushed by the warriors. In October 1675, the town of Springfield was burned to the ground. It was reported that Philip rewarded each of the leaders of the attacks with large quantities of wampum for their victories.

After years of being intimidated by the colonists of Plymouth, Massachussetts, and Rhode Island over border conflicts on their land, the Nipmucks were finally retaliat-

In the fall of 1675, the Nipmucks ambushed a series of New England towns. One of their most successful attacks was on the town of Springfield, which the Indians burned to the ground.

ing. When Philip's brother-in-law, Tuspaquin, a very powerful man who was both a powwow and the sachem of the Assawampsetts, joined the cause, the Nipmucks and Wampanoags rejoiced. Because of his spiritual power, it was widely believed that Tuspaquin could not be killed. Later, the death of many powwows would challenge the Indians' traditional belief in their leaders' invulnerability. But at the outset of the war, their beliefs gave them courage and confidence. In addition, Cautantowwit, and the promise of his heaven in the Southwest, was a strong source of motivation for the Indians as they fought for their homeland.

Not all of the Christian Indians joined the war. Many remained in their missions even as surrounding areas were set aflame by their non-Christian brothers. But the colonists came to mistrust all Indians in the months following the outbreak of attacks. They regarded the individual battles as an all-encompassing race war. In their anger, the colonists sent many friendly mission Indians to concentration camps located on two islands in Boston Harbor. Most of these Indians remained there with few provisions until near the end of the war.

Although Philip successfully recruited allies from across New England, he still had no luck convincing the Narragansetts to join with him. And Philip was not the only one who hoped to gain their support. When the war first broke out, representatives from Massachusetts and Connecticut raced to meet with the Narragansetts' mighty sachems. If Plymouth won the war, these colonies also wanted a share of Wampanoag land and would therefore benefit by keeping the Narragansetts out of the war.

Because they did not have an army of their own, the Rhode Island colonists were also afraid of the Narragansetts' neighbors. They knew that both the Massachusetts and Connecticut forces came to confront

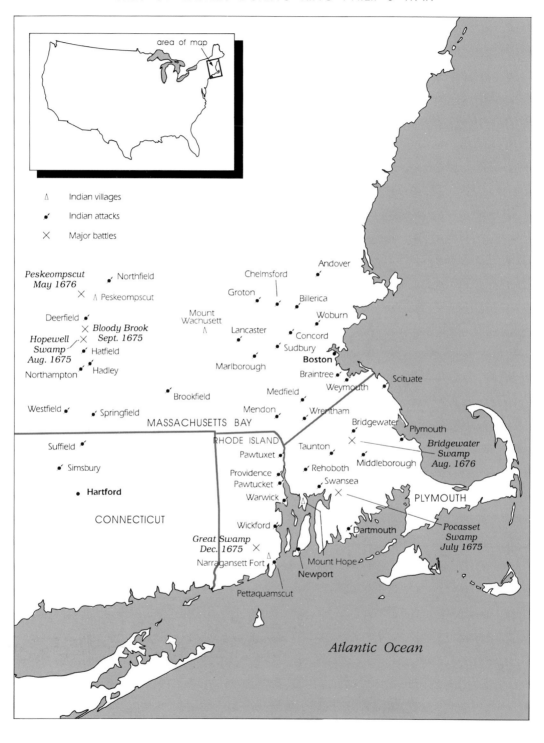

SITES OF BATTLES DURING KING PHILIP'S WAR

Λ   Indian villages

⚈   Indian attacks

✕   Major battles

Peskeompscut
May 1676 ✕   Λ Peskeompscut   Northfield

Deerfield

✕ *Bloody Brook*
   Sept. 1675
Hopewell ✕
Swamp   Hatfield
Aug. 1675
Northampton   Hadley

Westfield   Springfield

Suffield

Simsbury

Hartford

CONNECTICUT

Chelmsford
Groton
Mount
Wachusett
Λ   Lancaster

Marlborough

Brookfield

Mendon

Andover

Billerica
Woburn

Concord
Sudbury
Boston
Braintree
Weymouth   Scituate
Medfield
Wrentham
Bridgewater   Plymouth
✕   *Bridgewater*
Swamp
Aug. 1676

MASSACHUSETTS BAY

RHODE ISLAND
Pawtuxet
Providence
Pawtucket
Warwick

Taunton
Rehoboth   Middleborough
Swansea
✕
PLYMOUTH

Wickford   Dartmouth
Great Swamp
Dec. 1675 ✕
Narragansett Fort   Λ
Mount Hope
Newport

Pocasset
Swamp
July 1675

Pettaquamscut

Atlantic Ocean

area of map

the Narragansetts because they wanted to take more land from the Indians. Being Quakers, the Rhode Islanders did not believe in force as a viable means of negotiation. But they feared the outcome of a meeting between the colonial forces and the Narragansetts because they disapproved of violence and also because they thought of some of the land in question as their own.

With two armies at their doorstep, some of the minor Narragansett sachems were forced to sign a treaty agreeing not to give sanctuary to any Indian whose tribe was at war with the United Colonies. A bounty was placed on the heads of all Wampanoags. As usual, the Rhode Islanders stood behind the Indians, testifying to their honesty and their trustworthiness in negotiations. But before the primary sachems could be summoned to sign the agreement, the representatives from Massachusetts and Connecticut withdrew. The Connecticut soldiers were needed at home to prevent New York troops from entering western Connecticut lands while the Massachusetts troops were called back to stop Philip and the Nipmucks, who were setting frontier towns ablaze.

On August 15, near Philip's homeland, Captain Samuel Mosely confronted about 300 Indians with a company of approximately 60 swashbuckling mercenaries, including a group of pirates who had been released from death row in Boston and some ferocious slave-hunting dogs. Enlisted by Massachusetts Bay colonists, the buccaneers were guaranteed all of the plunder and captives that they could take. According to legend, when Mosely removed his wig and placed it in his breeches to allow him to fight more effectively, the Indians began "howling and yelling." Afraid of battling an enemy that had two heads, the Indians quickly fled across the fields.

In September, the news of war had spread to the northern Abenaki Indian tribes, including the Kennebecs and Penobscots. They had spent years harboring feelings of resentment and hostility toward the unjust and deceitful behavior of the English settlers, and the battles in southern New England spurred these northern tribes to fight back against their colonial oppressors. There was a series of surprise attacks against the frontier towns of present-day Maine and New Hampshire. Falmouth was abandoned and Scarborough was burned to the ground. With guns obtained from the French, Indians attacked the new communities vigorously. It was time they paid for stripping the ancestral forests and decimating the land.

Through it all, the Narragansetts still refused to don their war paint. They continued to avoid the ongoing slaughter between the other tribes and the colonists. Instead they built a fort in the depths of seemingly impenetrable swamps, where they hoped to remain safe from harm.

Then, in October 1675, Connecticut claimed that the Narragansetts had become allies of the Wampanoags. By this time, word was out that some of Philip's tribespeople were now living with the Narragansetts, and although they were mostly women and children, the colonists found it sufficient reason to launch an attack. Even though the Narragansett sachem, Pessacus, had delivered the heads of seven of Philip's men for bounty, on August 8, 1675, John Winthrop, Jr., governor of Connecticut, decided that an attack was essential to ensure his colony's interests. Nearby settlers fled from the region in fear of a violent outbreak.

In fact, there were several motives for the subsequent slaughter. The Rhode Islander William Harris had complained to the king's court in England about the disturbances in the colonies and asked for the king's assistance. Winthrop and the Connecticut leaders knew that if the war did not end soon, royal troops might well be sent to bring it to an end. If that happened, the Connecticut colonists could lose the chance to capture land desired by both themselves and the unarmed Rhode Islanders. It seemed in their best interest to attack quickly, claim the land they wanted, and end the war before the king sent troops.

Another report in the *London Gazette* helped to reveal a different motivation for their actions. The Narragansetts were supposedly harboring Weetamoo. And the colonists felt that "if she be taken by the *English*, her Lands will more than pay all Charge we have been at in this unhappy War."

Weeks before, the Narragansett sachem Canonchet had signed an agreement to hand over all of the Wampanoags to the colonists. In return he was given a silver-laced coat as a sign of friendship. When he was later asked to hand over Weetamoo and the Wampanoags, all of whom were sure to be executed or sold off as slaves in the West Indies, Canonchet flatly replied: "No, not a Wampanoag, nor the paring of a Wampanoag's nail." On November 2, 1675, the United Colonies declared war on the Narragansetts. Canonchet withdrew with his tribe deep into the swamp.

To achieve their goals, the Puritans and Pilgrims together mobilized a force of more than 1,000 men under the direction of General Josiah Winslow of Plymouth. It was the largest force ever mounted in New England. On December 18, the soldiers marched from Wickford through deep snows into Narragansett country. The soldiers hoped to catch the Narragansetts off guard—an unethical move by Algonkian standards because it offered the tribe no chance to hide its women and children. Arriving at a deserted Narragansett village, the hungry soldiers eagerly unearthed the Indians' winter supply of grain. As the soldiers ate, snow began to fall.

The swamps, frozen over and free of mosquitoes and rattlesnakes, now presented fewer problems to the advancing colonists. However, the English leaders had no

The English scored a major victory in their attack on a Narragansett fort in December 1675. Like the Pequot massacre 38 years earlier, this battle — now known as the Great Swamp Fight — resulted in the death of hundreds of Indian women and children.

idea where to turn in search of the missing Narragansetts. Then by chance they caught a Narragansett scout named Indian Peter. Under the threat of hanging, he revealed the location of a fort on a five-acre island in the middle of the swamp. The frightened scout claimed that not only the Narragansetts but also Philip and his warriors were hidden there.

Although other scouts alerted the Narragansetts that the army was on its way, they were too late. The first colonists that approached the opening of the fort were shot down. But then a large number of invaders rushed in and began to torch the wigwams inside. Later, this battle was called the Great Swamp Fight. The colonists set fire to 500 Narragansett wigwams and killed hundreds of unarmed women and children. Like the Pequot massacre 38 years earlier, this vulnerable group of noncombatants made up most of the victims. More than 600 Narragansetts were killed, and about 300 were taken prisoner. But, unlike the Pequot massacre, this time the

English also suffered extensive losses. The English lost 207 of their own soldiers, and had it not been for a ship from Boston that arrived to carry many of them away, more of the colonists would have died.

Benjamin Church pleaded with his commanders to stop. But they ignored him. Although Philip was not at the fort, some warriors did find him later and fight at his side, but they were few. Those who survived the slaughter were sent to the West Indies as slaves. Increase Mather wrote of them:

> When they came to see the ashes of their friends, mingled with the ashes of their fort . . . where the English had been doing a good day's work, they Howl'd, they Roar'd, they stamp'd, they tore their hair; . . . and were the pictures of so many *Devils* in Desperation.

Having fought poorly during most of the war, the English were satisfied with their attack on the Narragansetts. Without remorse, the Puritan leaders claimed that the gruesome massacre was in response to the Indians' fierce manner of fighting. But the English had also shown a cruel streak when fighting the Scots and the Irish during this time. During the Puritan Revolution, the English even brutally tortured men and women within their own communities.

Roger Williams reported in his early notes on the Narragansetts that mass slaughter was not common among the Indian tribes:

> Their Warres are farre lesse bloudy and devouring then the cruell Warres of Europe; and seldom twenty slaine in a pitcht filed . . . and yet having no Swords, nor Guns, all that are slaine are commonly slain with great Valour and Courage: for the Conquerour ventures into the thickest, and brings away the Head of his Enemy.

In the eyes of the Narragansetts, there were now many enemy heads waiting to be carried away.

A map from William Hubbard's History of the Indian Wars in New England. *The towns with numbers beside their name suffered Indian attacks during King Philip's War.*

8

INDIAN WARS

When the small band of Narragansett warriors approached, Philip's men prepared to fire at them. They trembled at the thought of having to fight the entire Narragansett nation as well as the colonists. But one of the Narragansetts signaled for them to hold their fire. Philip's men realized that none of them had fired a shot.

Philip and the Wampanoags accepted the news of the massacre solemnly. But they were glad that the Narragansetts had at last abandoned their neutral position and joined the battle against the cutthroats, a name reserved for the colonists as well as their pigs. Ironically, in their efforts to prevent a Narragansett-Wampanoag alliance, the colonists had in effect caused it to happen.

Deputy Governor John Easton of Rhode Island felt bad about his role in the affair. He had worked hard to convince the Narragansetts to remain neutral, reassuring them that if they did not enter battle with the English they would be spared in the war. Now it appeared that he had deceived them.

This time the Indians did not spare his colony. Providence and the surrounding towns were attacked. The Indians first raided Warwick, Rehoboth, Seekonk, and Wickford. By the end of the winter, they had also won battles at Chelmsford, Andover, and Haverhill. The united band of warriors set fire to 103 of the 123 houses in Providence.

Both sides suffered greatly through the winter. The colonists fell ill from lack of food and exposure to the cold. Indian attacks forced farmers and tradesmen, such as millwrights and blacksmiths, to abandon their work. Many of their crops and workshops were burned down or left unattended when the men went off to join the military. Fields lay barren across New England. Increase Mather sent letters to the governments of Ireland and England, begging for aid. The governments responded with both money and "a ship laden with provision" to help the poor of New England affected by the war.

The Indians' superior fighting tactics were taking a toll on the colonies. In a few months, they had completely decimated seven towns, and Maine was almost entirely lost. Indian scouts watched the frontier towns closely and determined the best time to strike. When they could see that the towns' defenders were outnumbered, the northern Indians would rush in, sometimes killing as few as one or two colonists. They scalped their victims and then retreated back into the forests before English reinforcements could arrive. An estimated 300 English soldiers were killed during such raids.

The Puritans blamed their mounting losses on their failure to please God. As the snow fell across New England, they huddled in their meetinghouses, despondently imploring God to come to their aid. Ministers were quick to blame the destruction on "the Apostacy of many from the Truth unto Heresies, and pernicious Errours . . . inordinate Affection and sinful Conformity to this present evil vain World."

Incredibly, it seemed not to cross the minds of the colonists that a revised practice in Indian relations might have lessened the viciousness of the war. In fact, the idea

Although the Pilgrims left England to escape religious persecution, they often were profoundly intolerant of beliefs and behavior not found in their strict moral code. Religious repression in Plymouth increased after clergyman Increase Mather interpreted the Indians' attacks as evidence of God's displeasure with the colonists and recommended enacting harsher laws "for the suppressing of sin."

that their unfair actions might have had something to do with the war was never even mentioned in their chronicles. Instead, further religious repression, especially against the Quakers, and stricter moral codes forbidding, among other things, fancy dress and idleness were enforced. Increase Mather, stirred by the belief that the attacks were somehow administered by the sword of God, preached for new laws to be passed in the colony. He was glad to report that "several wholesome laws for the surpressing of sin were thereupon made and published."

Some attempts at treaties were made, but the warfare was in general relentless. Any attack on the Indians, whether they were friendly, hostile, or neutral, was seen as an attack on Philip himself and therefore considered just and right. No one proved up to the task of negotiating between the forces. Only Rhode Island maintained its neutral stance, and the colony became a sanctuary: All white refugees were promised land and a cow, and all Indians were offered protection against being sold into slavery.

Although few of the Indian tribes took advantage of this offer, they too suffered through the winter. Without the stores of corn they usually reserved in the summer, many were low on food. But their superior hunting and survival skills helped them stave off starvation. Unlike the English, who seemed to fear the wilderness, the Indians lived in harmony in the forests. In addition, the Narragansetts' harvest had not been interrupted that year, so when they joined the others, more stores of food became available.

Nevertheless, warriors across New England saw defeat against the well-armed English as inevitable. The colonists seemed to have an endless supply of guns and gunpowder, and whereas the Indians had mastered the ability to use the weapons, their ammunition was scarce. Though Philip had proved capable of recruiting allies, he could not maintain a united front. He had served as a catalyst for the uprising, but his control over the war was much more limited than the colonists believed. Many warriors had not seen their family or homeland for over six months. Some began to speak of surrender.

Many diseases brought over by the colonists, including dysentery, measles, syphilis, and typhus, were afflicting large numbers of Indians. By 1675, The Algonkian Indians had been ravaged by disease. Of the estimated 70,000 to 100,000 Indians in New England in 1600, less than 20,000 remained. In contrast, there were already 50,000 colonists in the region.

In the face of such daunting odds, Philip decided to make a bold attempt at finding more allies. He refused to take part in any talk of defeat. Even though the snow was falling and the ground was frozen, the innovative sachem decided to take a trip to the north. There he hoped to convince the northern Mahicans and perhaps even the Abenaki to join his cause in the war.

Philip traveled quickly through the cold northern forests. He knew that the Mahicans had harbored many of the Pequots who had escaped when their tribe was slaughtered so many years ago. He hoped that at least these tribesmen and their descendants would understand the urgency of his plea.

Arriving at Schaghticoke, in present-day New York State, Philip was successful in recruiting not only the Mahicans but also many other warriors from nearby tribes. As the Mahicans and some northern Abenaki Indians gathered around him, Philip felt confident that at last he had a force that could destroy the colonies.

Meanwhile, the Connecticut colonists were trying to convince Governor Sir Edmund Andros of New York to send his Indian allies, the vast Mohawk nation, to fight Philip while he was within their reach. At first, Andros scoffed at their plea. Just a few months ago, Connecticut had refused his aid in the uprising and even sent troops to meet his soldiers at the border of Connecticut. The Connecticut colonists had considered his generous offer to be a ploy to get some of their land after the war.

Despite his reluctance to help Connecticut and the rest of New England, Andros did have his own colony to protect. When war first broke out, Andros and the Mohawks reinforced their relationship with a peace treaty to keep them both out of the war. However, if Philip continued to recruit Indian allies, Andros knew the war could spread to his colony and beyond. The governor stalled as long as he could, but when he received an exaggerated report from one of his scouts that Philip was seen with 2,100 Algonkians as well as a few hundred

Abenaki Indians, Andros realized that this was a force he could not well ignore.

Finally, he encouraged the Mohawks to attack Philip and destroy his forces. The Mohawks, having been in conflict with the northern Algonkian tribes for almost twenty years, planned to ambush their old enemies. Andros supplied them with weapons and sanctuary for their women and children against any possible retaliation by Philip.

The Mohawks' fierce attack was indeed a surprise to Philip and his new allies. He was devastated by this outside interference after having just proved his ability to negotiate and enlist fresh support. Philip's new force was beaten by the raging Mohawks, who were armed by Governor Andros and his colony. Many of his new allies fled for their homes in fear of further raids. Philip, dispirited by his loss and the betrayal of the Mohawks, was left with only a handful of warriors. In fear for his life, he retreated and started out on the long path home.

In the middle of February, Indian forces raided the town of Lancaster, which the Boston colonists had refused to defend. They stole into the town at sunrise. After burning most of the buildings, including the meeting-house, they took a woman named Mary Rowlandson captive. The raid was part of a major Indian offensive, one of the largest in the war. In the account of her captivity, which would become the most widely published nonreligious book of the 17th and 18th centuries, she wrote: "Thus we were butchered by those merciless Heathen, standing amazed, with the blood running down to our heels."

But Rowlandson survived. While other hysterical captives, screaming and complaining, were tortured and killed, Rowlandson became a loyal servant to Weetamoo and her third husband, the Narragansett sachem Quin-

A 20th-century depiction of English settler Mary Rowlandson being taken captive following an Indian raid on the town of Lancaster. In an account of her three years of captivity, she remembered King Philip as being kind and gentle.

napin. Her ability to do needlework proved useful to the Indians. Forced to travel with "master" throughout New England, Rowlandson met Philip in Coasset, Vermont, on his return from his disappointing trip to Schaghticoke.

The captive had no bitter words for the man that most colonists blamed for the start of the war. Although she took greatest comfort in God "and His goodness in bringing to my hand so many comfortable and suitable scriptures in my distress," Philip's gentleness and kindness of spirit can be glimpsed in her casual mention of him in her book: "Then I went to see King Philip, he

bade me come in and sit down, and asked me whether I would smoke [tobacco] (a usual Complement nowadayes amongst Saints and Sinners) but this no way suited me." After paying Rowlandson a shilling to make a shirt for his son, Philip invited the captive to have dinner with him. Rowlandson sat down with the sachem and ate "a pancake, about as big as two fingers. It was made of parched wheat, beaten, and fried in bear's grease, but I thought I had never tasted pleasanter meat in all my life."

When Rowlandson wrote about the Indians, she had difficulty explaining their victories. It was hard for her to comprehend how they could escape from the heavily armed colonists. Although the Indians' swiftness and the colonists' inexperience may have been reason enough, Rowlandson believed that the Indians were to be protected by the "providence of God."

Although Philip's dreams of a united Indian front against New England were devastated when the Mohawks destroyed his forces, the colonists in small frontier settlements could take little comfort in those distant victories. The Puritans suffered attacks on 52 of their 90 settlements in New England. A dozen of those settlements had been completely razed to the ground. For the settlers there, the threat of annihilation by the Indians was still very real.

Both sides were fighting with increasing vigor when spring arrived. Coastal towns were flooded with refugees from villages that had been destroyed. Terrified men who dreaded trudging through Indian-infested swamps tried desperately to avoid being drafted into the military.

At the same time, the Mohawks continued to raid the Algonkian tribes, slaughtering Philip's allies and taking many captives, who were burned at the stake in Mohawk villages. Many Indians already believed the cause was lost. Shoshanim, an important Nipmuck sachem who was known to the colonists as Sagamore Sam, argued with Philip that the hostages they held should be released to limit the potential retaliation of the colonists if the Indians lost the war. Knowing that his fate, as well as that of the majority of fighting Indians, would already be sealed if he was captured alive, Philip argued that it was best to keep the captives. That way they could retain more bargaining power if they were surrounded by the colonists.

In exchange for some goods, Sagamore Sam later released his captives to the colonial forces. But Philip's instincts proved correct. Sagamore Sam was captured and executed by the colonists. Philip had understood that the colonists had no compassion for him or for any Indians involved in the war.

In April, Canonchet was captured and charged with breaking his promise to fight against the Wampanoags. With a great number of warriors, he had been one of the primary leaders in the war, his military skills surpassing even those of Philip himself. The mighty sachem held his tongue in front of the colonists, who were of insufficient rank to address him, being mere subjects to the English crown. According to Boston clergyman William Hubbard, when he heard of his upcoming execution, he claimed he "liked it well that he should die before his heart was soft or he had spoken words unworthy of himself." At Stonington, he was shot by the Mohegan sachem Oneco and two Pequot sachems, as he requested. The last major Indian offensive was launched later that month. On April 21, a united Indian force attacked the town of Sudbury. It was a strategic move on the Indians' part, because the town was located on the road to Boston. The assault was a success at first, but the noise and smoke from the attack alerted colonists throughout the area. Two Christian Indians had previously spied on the Indian camp at Menamaset and warned the Boston colonists that the Indians hoped to attack their city in a major offensive.

Soldiers arrived from the neighboring towns, and a bitter battle ensued. Although the Indians killed over 70 colonists that day, they lost over 100 of their own. Their plans for waylaying Boston had been crushed. After this battle, only individual Indian efforts were pursued.

Philip met up with Mary Rowlandson again later that month. Physically exhausted and in a deep state of despair, she was struggling to keep up with her captors. Philip came to her aid, and once again she wrote of his gentleness:

> Going along, having indeed my life, but little Spirit, Philip, who was in the Company, came up and took me by the hand, and said Two weeks more and you shal [be] mistres again. I asked him if he spake true? he answered, Yes, and quickly you shal come to your master again; who had been gone from us three weeks.

The Indian sachems discussed how much they would ask for Rowlandson's ransom. Philip requested 2 coats, 20 shillings, a half bushel of corn, and some tobacco for himself. But when the decision was made to release her, he withdrew from the group. Even minor decisions were now beyond his control. Mary Rowlandson, having traveled with the Indians for almost three months, was released on May 2, 1676.

The war continued to consume New England despite the fact that the Indian forces were badly fragmented. On May 11, Tuspaquin and his men burned down 11 houses in Plymouth. Then, a week later, a devastating blow was dealt against the Indians. Captain William Turner, hearing of a large group of unguarded Indians gathered along the Connecticut River, brought together

*The title page of a 1676
English account of King
Philip's War. The text cites
the "Quarrelsome Disposition"
of the "Barbarous and Savage
Indian Natives" as the cause
of the conflict. The notion that
the colonists' conduct contrib-
uted to the outbreak of war
appears nowhere in English
chronicles of the fighting.*

A farther Brief and True

NARRATION

OF THE LATE

VVARS

RISEN IN

New - England,

Occasioned by the Quarrelsome Disposition and Perfidious
Carriage of the *Barbarous and Savage* Indian Natives there.

With an Account of the **FIGHT**,
the 19th of *December* laſt, 1675.

London, *February* 17th, 167⅘.
Licenſed,
Henry Oldenburg.

London, Printed by *J. D.* for *M. K.* and are to be Sold
by the Bookſellers, 1 6 7 6.

a force of more than 100 volunteers from Hadley,
Hatfield, and North Hampton. They attacked the Indians
at Peskeompskut, on the banks of the river. Consisting
mostly of women and children, many of the group were
killed as they tried to race from colonial bullets toward
the safety of the water.

The numerous Indian offenses of the early spring had tapered off to a trickle of raids by late May. Some tribes, afraid of Puritan retaliation in the event of their defeat, fled to New York, where Governor Andros offered sanctuary. After the battle at Peskeompskut, those Indians who survived raced to New York to take refuge from both the attacking Mohawks and the Connecticut colonists. Even after the war ended, the United Colonies continued to call upon Andros to turn the Algonkians over to them. The New York governor adamantly refused, and 25 years later, the refugees were still singing his praise.

Other tribes met with representatives of the colonies. In June, Wannalancet, sachem of the Pennacooks, arrived at Dover, New Hampshire, to reestablish good relations with the English. A large number of Indians to the north also quickly aligned themselves with the English. Even more damaging to Philip and his allies, the Christian Indians then entered the war. After months of cruel treatment in concentration camps, they were released to help fight their heathen brothers. Daniel Gookin, now a captain in the Massachusetts Bay militia, claimed that it was these 60 or so Indians from Boston who "turned ye balance to ye English side."

In the north, the Mohawks continued to strike again and again. Inspired by their bloody assaults, the colonists began to attack more fiercely. If they had ever doubted that God was on their side, their renewed courage on the battlefield proved to them that they had his wholehearted support.

Each of the colonies struggled to get the upper hand in the war. As Indian leaders throughout the region offered to negotiate, the English insisted on nothing less than unconditional surrender. However, complete surrender meant certain death or enslavement for the Indian leaders and their tribespeople.

When attacking villages, the colonists killed Indian women and children without mercy, often murdering them in their sleep. On July 2, a Connecticut force led by John Talcott assaulted a Narragansett tribe in Rhode Island consisting of 34 men and 137 women. All of the men were killed, as well as 92 of the women and children. On the following day, Talcott interfered with peace negotiations at Newport and once again slaughtered a large number of Narragansetts. By the end of the day, the colonists had killed, or captured, 67 more Indians.

Feeling compelled to justify the viscious treatment of the Indians at this point in the war, Roger Williams wrote a letter to Governor John Winthrop:

> I presume you are satisfied in the necessity of these present hostilities, and that it is not possible at present to keep peace with these barbarous men of blood, who are justly repelled and subdued as wolves that assault sheep. . . . I fear the event of the justest war.

Although he was now only a minor leader in a battle that seemed all but lost, Philip insisted on complete resistance to the end. With nowhere else to turn, he began a journey back to his native Mount Hope.

9

▿▿▿

HEARTBROKEN

Benjamin Church realized that he would need to recruit more Indian scouts to help him track down the elusive Philip. Close to his home at Little Compton, he arranged a meeting with the Sakonnet sachem Awashonks and brought with him some tobacco and a large gourd filled with rum. As they sat down together, Awashonks was reluctant to drink from the gourd. Fearing Church's treachery, she and her counselors decided not to take the rum, suspecting that it was poisoned.

They waited for Church to drink first. After Church casually took a few mouthfuls of rum, the Sakonnets were convinced. Anashonks "ventured to take a good hearty dram," and they all proceeded to drink with Church long into the night. The captain promised the Sakonnets not only more rum but also many other goods if they would help him capture Philip. As was the case throughout the war, the thought of booty was enticing. And, by the end of the night, Awashonks had agreed.

According to William Hubbard, who wrote an account of the war entitled *History of the Indian Wars in New England*, Philip was deeply hurt by the news that Awashonks had joined Captain Church against him. Hubbard recorded that "this Act of these Indians broke *Philip's* Heart as soon as he ever understood it, so as he never joyed after, or had any Success in any of his Designs, but lost his Men one Time after another."

An engraving from the 19th century of the assassination of King Philip.

With Awashonks' scouts to help him, Church pursued Philip in earnest. He was confident, both in the loyalty of his Indian allies and in the crumbled power of his enemy. That summer, he employed Indian warfare techniques and was much more successful than he had been in earlier efforts. As his men advanced through the woods, they kept a good distance between them to avoid being caught in the tight circle of an Indian ambush.

On July 30, 1676, Church chased Philip from the Massachusetts Bay Colony town of Bridgewater into the swamps of Norton and Rehoboth. In a skirmish beside the Taunton River, Philip's uncle Unkompoin was killed. The same day, Philip lost his family. His wife, Wootonekanuska, his son, and many other Wampanoags were captured by the colonists and brought to Plymouth for trial. Weetamoo was found drowned in the Taunton River on August 3.

Wherever Philip sought refuge, he discovered that Church had captured more of his followers. In one bold move, 130 Indians were caught unaware by Church's much smaller force. A Christian Indian named Mathias warned them in their language that if they shot their guns, they would be killed. The Wampanoags were so shocked that they did not fire and surrendered up to the army. Philip's family was being held captive by the English, most of his friends were gone, and his tribespeople had been slaughtered. Yet Philip was incapable of relinquishing power to the settlers.

Church and his combined forces moved stealthily into Wampanoag territory. Church stopped briefly to surprise his wife, who was staying at the house of Major Peleg Sanford. There, Major Sanford interrupted their reunion with important news. Philip had arrived at Mount Hope with a small group of men.

The Indian who reported Philip's arrival at Mount Hope to Church had good reason for informing on his sachem. Days before, his brother had suggested to Philip that he make peace with the colonists, and the exhausted and tense sachem had killed him on the spot.

On the night of August 11, Church's men advanced toward Mount Hope. They had planned a surprise attack for dawn the next day, but it was spoiled when a gun went off in the woods. The sleeping Wampanoags were soon awake and on the alert. As Philip ran toward the nearby swamp, he was confronted by a Pocasset named Alderman and a colonist named Cook. Cook misfired, but Alderman shot two musket balls through the heart of the approaching sachem. William Hubbard wrote of Philip's demise:

> Philip, like a Savage and wild Beast, having been hunted by the English forces through the Woods . . . at last was driven to his own Den, upon *Mount-hope*, where retiring himself with a few of his best Friends into a Swamp, which proved but a Prison to keep him fast, till the Messengers of Death came by Divine Permission to execute Vengeance upon him, which was thus accomplished.

Terwileema, shown here in an 1885 photograph, was King Philip's last female descendant.

Church ordered Philip's head to be chopped off and his body quartered. An Indian executioner performed the grisly rite. Philip's head and one of his hands were saved; his quartered body was strewn about in the nearby trees. The head was placed on display in Plymouth, where it remained for at least 20 years. The hand was given to Alderman, who exhibited it for many years—to anyone willing to pay a good price.

Increase Mather's son, Cotton, triumphantly wrote of the arrival of Philip's head at Plymouth: "Thus did God break the Head of that *Leviathan*, and give it to be Meat to the People inhabiting the Wilderness, and brought it to the Town of Plymouth, the very Day of their solemn Festival." He then left for Boston with a trophy for that city—Philip's lower jaw.

Wootonekanuska and her nine-year-old son were sold as slaves in Bermuda, despite missionary John Eliot's pleas for their freedom. Church tracked down Annawon a month later, the last of Philip's "best Friends" to remain at large.

Approximately 2,500 colonists died in the battles that would collectively come to be known as King Philip's War. Although the settlers were the victors, New England's expansion was halted for almost a century. The bodies of numerous men lay beneath unmarked graves in the forest. For months, perhaps years, afterward, hunting Indians became a popular sport.

A 1922 painting of King Philip by American artist Thomas Hart Benton.

The United Colonies gained very little land, considering all the blood that was spilled. Plymouth Colony was so weakened by the war that it was annexed by Massachusetts Bay 16 years later. Even Mount Hope and Sowams, where the war began, were taken over by Rhode Island and became the present-day towns of Bristol and Warren. Connecticut lost many of its disputes with Rhode Island over Narragansett lands as well.

But the toll suffered by the Indians was far more devastating. Six thousand Algonkians were wounded, dead, or enslaved. Almost all of the Indians' leaders were killed in battle or executed when captured. Other Indians were sold as slaves in the West Indies to help cover the costs of the war. The Indians' land was usurped. Although some Wampanoags did remain in and around Mount Hope, by 1686, all Indians were barred from hunting in the area.

Philip's determination and the colonists' aggression led to the the most destructive war in the history of New England. At this pivotal point in the history of colonial and Indian relations, not only was Philip killed, but most of his nation was destroyed as well. Whereas many Puritans may have been delighted by the annihilation of the Indians in New England, there were others, such as Benjamin Church and Mary Rowlandson, who sadly mourned their absence. Although they fought and prayed fervently for the Puritan cause, Church and Rowlandson recorded both their admiration for the skills of the Indians and their sympathy for the Indians' loss. By no means did either hope for the emptiness in the forests and in the hearts of those who inherited these lands, long after Philip and his people were gone.

KING PHILIP

CHRONOLOGY

ca. 1638	Metacom, son of Wampanoag sachem Massasoit, born
1660	Massasoit dies; Wamsutta, his eldest son, succeeds him as sachem; Metacom given the name Philip and Wamsutta the name Alexander
1662	Alexander dies on the way home from Plymouth; Philip becomes sachem of Wampanoags
Aug. 6, 1662	Signs agreement with Plymouth forbidding the sale of Wampanoag land to other colonies
1671	Armed Wampanoags parade in front of the frontier town of Swansea
April 10, 1671	Philip signs Treaty of Taunton, relinquishing 70 of his men's weapons
Sept. 1671	Once again called to Plymouth; forced to declare complete subjugation to the colonists
Jan. 1675	Body of John Sassamon discovered in Assawompsett Pond
June 8, 1675	Three Wampanoags executed for the murder of Sassamon
June 17, 1675	Philip and 40 of his men meet with John Easton at Trip's Ferry; attempt to negotiate peace settlement
June 30, 1675	Philip flees Montaup; Benjamin Church and colonial army chase him
Sept.–Oct. 1675	Towns throughout New England attacked by alliance of Wampanoags, Nipmucks, and other Indian tribes
Dec. 18, 1675	Great Swamp Fight between combined force of United Colonies and Narragansetts
Jan.–Feb. 1676	Philip recruits Mahicans and other northern allies to Indian cause; in a surprise attack, Mohawks destroy new forces
April 11, 1676	Narragansett sachem Canonchet, one of the most important leaders of the war, captured and later executed
April 21, 1676	Attack on Sudbury, last major Indian assault of the war
June 1676	Awashonks pledges to assist in capturing Philip
Aug. 11, 1676	Philip shot, decapitated, and quartered at Montaup

FURTHER READING

Bourne, Russell. *The Red King's Rebellion: Racial Politics in New England 1675–1678*. New York: Atheneum, 1990.

Church, Benjamin. *Diary of King Philip's War, 1675–76*. Chester, CT: Pequot Press, 1975.

Cwiklik, Robert. *King Philip and the War with the Colonists*. Englewood Cliffs, NJ: Silver Burdett, 1989.

Horowitz, David. *The First Frontier: The Indian Wars and America's Origins, 1607–1776*. New York: Simon & Schuster, 1978.

Jennings, Francis. *The Invasion of America: Indians, Colonialism and the Cant of Conquest*. Chapel Hill: University of North Carolina Press, 1975.

Leach, Douglas Edward. *Flintlock and Tomahawk; New England in King Philip's War*. New York: Norton, 1966.

Nash, Gary B. *Red, White and Black: The Peoples of Early America*. Englewood Cliffs, NJ: Prentice-Hall, 1974.

Slotkin, Richard, and James K. Folson, eds. *So Dreadful a Judgment: Puritan Responses to King Philip's War, 1676–1677*. Middletown, CT: Wesleyan University Press, 1978.

Webb, Stephen Saunders. *1676: The End of American Independence*. New York: Knopf, 1984.

Weinstein-Farson, Laurie. *The Wampanoag*. New York: Chelsea House, 1989.

INDEX

PICTURE CREDITS

JOSEPH ROMAN is a freelance writer living in New York.

W. DAVID BAIRD is the Howard A. White Professor of History at Pepperdine University in Malibu, California. He holds a Ph.D. from the University of Oklahoma and was formerly on the faculty of history at the University of Arkansas, Fayetteville, and Oklahoma State University. He has served as president of both the Western History Association, a professional organization, and Phi Alpha Theta, the international honor society for students of history. Dr. Baird is also the author of *The Quapaw Indians: A History of the Downstream People* and *Peter Pitchlynn: Chief of the Choctaws* and the editor of *A Creek Warrior of the Confederacy: The Autobiography of Chief G. W. Grayson.*